Grammaire

Unité 1
Décrire et s'exprimer dans le cadre de situations au présent

Les noms

- Les noms anglais sont soit dénombrables, soit indénombrables.
- Un nom dénombrable est un nom dont on peut dénombrer des unités (**one cat, two cats, three cats**) alors qu'un indénombrable est perçu comme une notion (ex. : **fruit**, *les fruits* en général, **furniture**, *les meubles* en général).
- Les indénombrables sont surtout les denrées alimentaires (ex. : **milk, tea, butter**, **bread, rice**, etc.) et les notions abstraites générales (**truth, love, happiness**). Beaucoup ne correspondent pas à nos représentations francophones (ex. : **hair, luggage, news**, voir Banque de mots). Il est possible de désigner une unité d'un indénombrable en employant ce qu'on appelle un dénombreur (ex. : **a glass of orange juice**, *un verre de jus d'orange*, **a piece of fruit**, *un fruit*).

	Articles, déterminants et accords

Dénombrables	- Au singulier : peuvent être précédés de **a/an, the, one** et de **the**, **Ø** ou d'un nombre au pluriel.
	  Ex. : **an apple, the apple, one apple, I like apples**
	- Pluriels irréguliers : **penny → pence, sheep → sheep, child → children, mouse → mice, tooth → teeth, foot → feet**
	Cas particuliers :
	- Les noms en **-ics** sont suivis d'un verbe au singulier.
	  Ex. : **physics, gymnastics is**, *la physique, la gymnastique est…*
	- Les noms collectifs comme **the team, the police** sont suivis d'un verbe au pluriel.
	  Ex. : **the team are motivated**, *l'équipe est motivée*
	- **Pyjamas, trousers, scissors** sont toujours au pluriel.
	  Ex. : **these trousers are warm**, *ce pantalon est chaud*
	- **Hundred, thousand** et **million** sont invariables quand précédés d'une unité. Ex. : **four hundred, six thousand, five million dollars**

Indénombrables	S'utilisent avec **the, Ø** ou un dénombreur. Attention à l'accord car si l'indénombrable se traduit parfois en français par un pluriel, le nom est singulier en anglais. Ex. : **fruit is sweet**, *les fruits sont sucrés*

Banque de mots

apricot ['èïprik^eut], *abricot*

asparagus [^eus'parag^eus], *asperge*

avocado [av^eu'kad^euou], *avocat*

beef ['bif], *bœuf*

bitter ['bit^eur], *acide*

bread ['brèd], *pain*

cereals ['si^euri^eulz], *céréales*

cheese ['tchiz], *fromage*

cherry ['tchèri], *cerise*

chip ['tchip], *frite*

clothing ['kl^euouDHing], *habits*

corn ['kôn], *maïs*

dairy ['dèri], *produits laitiers*

fizzy drinks ['fizi drinks], *sodas*

flavour ['flèïv^eur], *saveur*

freedom ['frid^eum], *liberté*

French beans ['frènch binz], *haricots verts*

fruit ['frout], *fruits*

grapefruit ['grèïpfrout], *pamplemousse*

grapes ['grèïps], *raisin*

ham ['Ham], *jambon*

honey ['Heuni], *miel*

lamb ['lam], *agneau*

leek ['lik], *poireau*

lemon ['lèm^eun], *citron*

lettuce ['lètis], *laitue*

life ['laïf], *vie*

mashed potatoes ['macht p^eu'tèït^euouz], *purée*

meat ['mit], *viande*

mushroom ['meuchr**ou**m], *champignon*

oil ['oïl], *huile*

paper ['pèïp^eur], *papier*

pasta ['past^eu], *pâtes*

peach ['pitch], *pêche*

pear ['pè^eur], *poire*

pepper ['pèp^eur], *poivre, poivron*

pineapple ['païnap^eul], *ananas*

plum ['pleum], *prune*

poultry ['pôltri], *volaille*

raspberry ['razb^euri], *framboise*

rice ['raïs], *riz*

salmon ['sâm^eun], *saumon*

salt ['sôlt], *sel*

seafood ['si fou**d**], *fruits de mer*

shrimp ['chrimp], *crevette*

sparkling water ['spâkling ouôt^eur], *eau gazeuse*

spices ['spaïsiz], *épices*

spinach ['spinitch], *épinards*

strawberry ['strôb^euri], *fraise*

sugar ['choug^eur], *sucre*

sweet ['souit], *doux, sucré*

truth ['trouTH], *vérité*

tuna ['tioun^eu], *thon*

vegetables ['vèdjt^eub^eulz], *légumes*

vinegar ['vinig^eur], *vinaigre*

waffle ['ouaf^eul], *gaufre*

watermelon ['ouôt^eumèl^eun], *pastèque*

1 Détache les mots au bon endroit et place-les à côté de la bonne illustration (s'ils en ont une !).

dairymeatshrimpgrapesplumwafflecornpearhamhoneyoilmushroompeachgrapefruitleek

 1.............. 2.............. 3.............. 4..............

 5.............. 6.............. 7.............. 8..............

2 Complète les phrases suivantes avec is et/ou are.

1. Genetics .... a complicated science.

2. My new jeans .... comfortable.

3. .... your fruit ripe?

4. Spinach .... not a food children generally like.

5. Your hair .... grey now.

6. The lemons .... not bitter enough.

7. The police .... arriving.

8. Wow, your pasta .... so good!

9. His suitcases .... heavy.

10. My luggage .... in the hall.

11. The sheep .... eating grass.

12. Ten million .... missing.

3 Corrige les erreurs éventuelles.

1. There's a mice in the cellar.
....

2. I have got three hundred books.
....

3. I would like one honey.
....

4. She's writing on a paper.
....

5. I love peaches.
....

6. I'm drinking a water.
....

7. Your pyjamas is dirty.
....

8. The team is ready for the game.
....

Classe les aliments suivants dans le tableau.

salmon, cherry, mashed potatoes, grapefruit, chips, rice, lamb, pasta, lettuce, apricot,
French beans, asparagus, ham, peach, watermelon, honey, pepper, tuna, strawberrry

vegetables	fruit	cereals	meat	seafood	condiments
....	....	....	....	....	....
....	....	....	....	....	....
....	....	....	....	....	....
....	....	....	....	....	....
....	....	....	....	....	....

La quantité

On l'indique à l'aide de quantifieurs. Voici les principaux :

Quantité	Dénombrables	Indénombrables
aucun / pas de	no, not any + N	no, not any
peu de	few	little
quelques / un peu de	a few	a little
du, de la, des	some à la FA, **any** aux FI et FN	some à la FA, **any** aux FI et FN
assez de	enough	enough
plusieurs	several	
beaucoup de	many, a lot of	much, a lot of
plein de	plenty of	plenty of
trop de	too many	too much
tout (le), tous (les)	every, each, all the - **every** + singulier - **each** + singulier = *chaque, chacun* - **all (the*)** + pluriel * On ajoute **the** quand il s'agit d'un groupe défini.	all the
combien ? quelle quantité ?	how many?	how much?

5 Complète les phrases avec **some** ou **any** (de 1 à 4) et par **much** ou **many** (de 5 à 8).

1. She'd like …… honey in her tea. She never takes …… sugar.

2. I don't put …… mushrooms in my sauce. I put …… onions.

3. Do you add …… salt in your soup?

4. There isn't …… dairy left in the fridge.

5. How …… shrimps does this recipe use?

6. How …… cheese do you want?

7. I always have …… seafood in the summer.

8. You never have too …… chips!

9. Hurry up. I don't have …… time.

10. Not …… people love spinach.

6 Entoure le (ou les) quantifieur(s) ou article(s) compatible(s).

1. There isn't …. orange juice.	a few	any	a little	some
2. We've got …. corn.	much	several	not any	many
3. How …. strawberries do you need?	much	many	a few	little
4. Give me …. oil, please.	any	a few	a little	every
5. There are …. waffles.	much	few	too much	enough
6. Don't put …. salt in the salad.	too many	some	too much	any
7. There is …. freedom in dictatorships.	few	no	little	too many
8. …. news do you have?	how much	how many		

7 Jules et sa copine passent 2 semaines de vacances avec leurs amis, ils font le bilan de ce qu'il leur reste dans le placard.

"We've got a little corn, enough ham for ten, several avocados, a lot of salmon, not enough dairy for ten, too much rice, a few pineapples, many plums, few leeks, a little honey, not any bread, plenty of raspberries, all the sparkling water we want."

Complète la grille suivante (mots en français).

Across (horiz.)
Ils en ont…

1. assez pour 10

6. à foison !

9. quelques-uns

10. trop

Down (vert.)
Ils en ont…

2. plusieurs

3. beaucoup (fruits rouges)

4. beaucoup (poisson)

5. un peu (condiment sucré)

7. pas du tout

8. un peu (légume)

FA = forme affirmative
FI = forme interrogative
FN = forme négative

Les deux présents

Le présent progressif

• Formation : **to be** + BV + **-ing**
  Ex. : **She's/We're reading**
  FA : **I am swimming**
  FI : **Is she swimming?**
  FN : **They are not swimming**

• Utilisation :
- pour une action qui se déroule
  au moment où l'on parle
  Ex. : **Look, she's reading!**
- pour une action ou état de fait valable
  temporairement
  Ex. : **She's reading today!**
- dans des situations d'énervement
  Ex. : **You're always reading!**
  Tu es tout le temps en train de lire !

Le présent simple

• Formation : BV à toutes les personnes,
  avec ajout de **-s** à la 3ᵉ pers. du sing.
  Ex. : **She reads / we read.**
  FA : **I swim well.**
  FI : **Does she swim well?**
  FN : **They do not swim well.**

• Utilisation :
- pour une action régulière
- un état permanent, une vérité générale
  Ex. : **Koalas live in Australia.**
- un proverbe
  Ex. : **Slow and steady wins the race**, *Rien
  ne sert de courir, il faut partir à point.*

- pour parler de
  ses habitudes, de ses
  goûts, activités et opinions
  Ex. : **I don't like painting / my sister
  thinks you're great!**
• Certains verbes ne se mettent qu'au présent simple : les verbes de perception
  (**see, hear**), de goût (**like, love, prefer,
  hate**), de volonté (**wish, want**) et de pen-
  sée (**believe, understand, know, think**),
  mais également **to feel** (*sentir, ressentir*),
  to mean (*signifier*), **to need** (*avoir besoin
  de*)**, to remember** (*se souvenir de*).

• Avec le présent simple, on utilise souvent des adverbes de fréquence (voir
  Banque de mots). Pour interroger sur
  la fréquence, on emploie **how often**.
  Ex. : **How often do you order pizzas?**
  *À quelle fréquence commandes-tu des
  pizzas ?*

• **NB :** La question **What do you do?** signifie *Que faites-vous dans la vie ?*

Banque de mots

Adverbes de fréquence

always ['ôlouèïz], *toujours*

every ['èvri] **day** ['dèï], **week** ['ouik], **month** ['meunTH], **year** [i^eur], *chaque jour, semaine, mois, année*

generally ['djènr^euli], *généralement*

hardly ever ['Hâdli 'èv^eur], *presque jamais*

never ['nèv^eur], *jamais*

occasionally [^eu'kèïj^eun^euli], *de temps en temps*

often ['of^eun], *souvent*

once ['oueuns], *une fois*

regularly ['règioul^euli], *régulièrement*

seldom ['sèld^eum], **rarely** ['rè^euli], *rarement*

sometimes ['seumtaïmz], *parfois*

three times ['THri 'taïms], *trois fois*

twice ['touaïs], *deux fois*

usually ['iouj^euli], *d'habitude*

Autres mots

abroad [^eu'br^euoud], *à l'étranger*

angry ['èngri], *en colère, énervé*

to argue ['âgiou], *se disputer*

asthma ['azm^eu], *asthme*

to believe (in) [bi'liv], *croire (en)*

to brush + possessif + **teeth** ['breuch … 'tiTH], *se brosser les dents*

cello ['tchèl^euou], *violoncelle*

to contain [k^eun'tèïn], *contenir*

country ['keuntri], *campagne*

crisps ['krisps], *chips*

decade ['dèkèïd], *décennie*

diary ['daï^euri], *journal intime*

to do ['dou], *faire*

to fall asleep ['fôl ^eu'slip], *s'endormir*

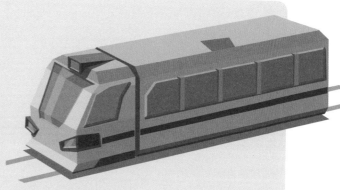

fat ['fat], *gros*

to fly ['flaï], *voler*

game console ['gèïm kon's^euoul], *console de jeux*

to hang about ['Hang ^euba-out], *traîner avec*

holidays ['Holidèïz], *vacances*

jewels ['djou^eulz], *bijoux*

to live ['liv], *vivre*

midnight ['midnaït], *minuit*

necklace ['nèkl^eus], *collier*

neighbour ['nèïb^eur], *voisin*

nurse ['neus], *infirmière*

oxygen ['oksidj^eun], *oxygène*

to shave ['chèïv], *se raser*

snack ['snak], *en-cas*

to stand ['stand], *se tenir*

to study ['steudi], *étudier*

step-father ['stèp fâDH^eur], *beau-père*

to take a bath [bâTH], *prendre un bain*

to take the underground ['tèïk DHi 'eund^eugra-ound], *prendre le métro*

tie ['taï], *cravate*

to want ['ouãt], *vouloir*

to wait ['ouèït], *attendre*

weak ['ouik], *faible*

to wear ['ouè^eur], *porter (un vêtement)*

8 Remets les lettres dans l'ordre puis indique à quelle image ça correspond.

1. UBRHS your EHTET ....

2. LALF PELASE ....

3. LYF ....

4. GAHN TOBUA ....

5. RAWE ....

6. ETKA A TABH ....

7. TEKA HET REGUDRONUND ....

8. VASHE ....

a.

b.

c.

d.

e.

f.

g.

h.

9 Corrige les erreurs éventuelles de temps.

1. "Time flies" is a proverb. It's meaning *"le temps passe (vite)"*.

....

2. Look Dad! John wears your tie.

....

3. My father hardly ever shaves.

....

4. My sister is wanting a chocolate bar.

....

5. What is your father doing? He's a doctor.

....

6. What do you do? I'm having lunch.

....

7. How often are you going to the swimming-pool?

....

10 Entoure le ou les nom(s) permettant de former une phrase pertinente.

1. I write in my *diary – cello – jewel*

2. We spend our holidays *abroad – in the country – midnight*

3. My sister plays the *necklace – diary – cello*

4. A necklace is a type of *tie – jewel – cello*

5. English students wear a *tie – diary – jewel*

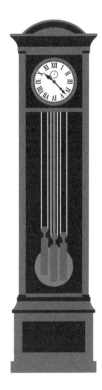

11 Conjugue les verbes au temps qui convient (présent simple ou présent continu).

1. I usually .... (to hang about) with my friends on Saturdays.

2. Tom .... (to live) with his father this week.

3. Oh no! You're .... (not eat) my waffle!

4. The Eiffel Tower .... (to stand) in Paris.

5. I always .... (walk) to school.

6. I .... (eat) fruit every day but today I .... (eat) junk food.

7. ...... you .... (to believe in) aliens?

12 En t'aidant des données ci-dessous et en utilisant un des adverbes de fréquence fournis, complète les phrases suivantes, qui évoquent les habitudes alimentaires de Tom.

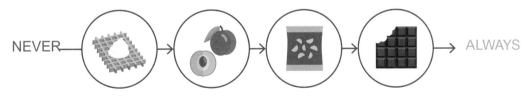

NEVER → → → → ALWAYS

usually, seldom, hardly ever, once a week

1. He .... has ....

2. He .... has ....

3. He .... has ....

4. He .... has ....

Banque de mots

(to be) all the same ['ôl DH^eu 'sèïm] **to someone**, *être égal à quelqu'un*

I can't stand [kãt 'stènd], *je ne supporte pas*

crosswords ['krosou**eu**dz], *mots croisés*

crazy about ['krèïzi ^eu'ba-out], *fou de quelque chose*

detective story [di'tèktiv stori], *roman policier*

to dig ['dig], *kiffer (familier)*

to dislike [dis'laïk], *ne pas aimer*

fairy tale ['fèri tèïl], *conte de fées*

favourite ['fèïvrit], *préféré*

jigsaw puzzle ['djigsô peuz^eul], *puzzle*

to loathe ['l^euouDH], *détester*

to not mind [not 'maïnd], *ne pas déranger*

novel ['neuv^eul], *roman*

poetry ['po^eutri], *poésie*

short story ['chôt stori], *nouvelle*

spicy food ['spaïsi 'fou**d**], *nourriture épicée*

yuck ['ieuk], *beurk*

yum ['ieum], *miam*

En t'aidant du tableau ci-dessous, entoure la ou les bonne(s) proposition(s), ou complète les phrases en ajoutant le prénom ou le nom qui convient.

1. Harriet *can't stand – doesn't mind* honey.

2. Vera *is crazy about – loathes - digs* cherries. They are her ……… fruit.

3. Tina thinks strawberries are okay. It's *all the same to her – her favourite fruit*. But she *dislikes – loathes* grapes.

4. Tina is crazy about ………

5. ……… doesn't mind mushrooms.

6. Tina says: '………, yum!'

7. Vera says: 'Leeks, ………!'

	😠	😐	🙂
Tina			
Vera			
Harriet			

Complète les cases suivantes (note que deux termes sont composés de deux mots séparés par un espace, qui compte comme une lettre).

Across (horiz.)

5. Histoire pour enfants : …….. ……

6. Le miel l'est

9. Un puzzle : **a ……….. puzzle**

10. Elle rime

11. Nouvelle (court roman)

Down (vert.)
Ils en ont…

1. Ouvrage comme *Madame Bovary* ou *Oliver Twist*

2. Eau avec des bulles :……… **water**

3. Le citron l'est.

4. Carrefour de mots.

7. Pour une glace par exemple, chocolat, fraise ou vanille en sont…

8. Un soda : **a ……. drink**

Choix et préférences

- Le choix s'exprime à l'aide de ces deux structures :
  - **either** ['aïDH^{eur}] **… or**, *ou bien … ou bien*
  Ex. : **You can have either an apple or a pear**
  - **neither** ['naïDH^{eur}] **… nor**, *ni … ni*
  Ex. : **I like neither apples nor pears**

- Pour exprimer une préférence, tu utiliseras le verbe **to prefer … to …**
  Ex. : **I prefer tea to coffee**, *Je préfère le thé au café*

15 Complète les espaces par **either, or, neither** ou **nor**.

1. I always have .... tea .... chocolate for breakfast, never coffee. But my husband likes .... coffee .... chocolate, so he usually has some tea.

2. My sister likes .... orange juice .... soda, so she always drinks .... sparkling water .... lemonade.

16 Construis des énoncés exprimant la préférence à partir des éléments suivants. Utilise le verbe **to prefer**.

1. Roger – saveurs sucrées < saveurs acides ....

2. My little brother – puzzles < mots croisés ....

3. Your little sister – puzzles < contes de fées..

4. My mother – romans policiers < poésie ....

Le gérondif

Un gérondif est un nom formé par l'ajout de la désinence **-ing** à une BV.

Ex. : **speak → speaking, move → moving**

Il s'emploie comme un nom normal ou comme un infinitif français (quand celui-ci peut être remplacé par l'expression *le fait de*).

Ex. : **laughing**, *le rire, le fait de rire*

Le gérondif peut avoir fonction de sujet.

Ex : **Laughing is good**, *Rire / Le fait de rire fait du bien*

Il peut également avoir fonction de complément.

Ex. : **I hate reading**, *Je déteste la lecture/lire*

On l'utilise pour :

• évoquer des activités de loisirs
  Ex. : **roller-skating**, *le roller*

• dans des expressions avec le verbe **to do**
  Ex. : **to do the shopping / the washing up / the cleaning**. *faire les courses / la vaisselle / le nettoyage*

• parler de ses goûts, après les verbes et expressions **to (dis)like, to love, to hate, to be keen on, to be crazy/mad about, to be fond of, to enjoy, to prefer (something to something), to feel like, to be interested in, I can't stand/bear, I don't mind, to be fed up with/sick of.**

• avant des structures servant à proposer une activité : **what about** [ouot ᵉᵘ' ba-out], **how about** ['Ha-ou ᵉᵘ'ba-out], *et si on ... ? pourquoi ne pas ...?*

Banque de mots

to be afraid of [ᵉᵘ'frèïd ᵉᵘv], *avoir peur de*

band ['band], *groupe*

bike ['baïk], *vélo*

bowling ['bᵉᵘouling], *bowling*

camping ['kamping], *le camping*

I can't stand/bear [kãt 'stand/bèᵉᵘr], *je ne supporte pas*

choir ['kouaïᵉᵘr], *chorale*

to be crazy/mad about ['krèïzi/mad ᵉᵘ'baout], *être fou de*

I don't mind ['maïnd], *ça ne me dérange pas*

drums ['dreumz], *batterie*

to dust ['deust], *faire la poussière*

to enjoy [in'djoï], *bien aimer, apprécier*

to be fed up ['fèd ᵉᵘp] **with / sick of** ['sik ᵉᵘv], *en avoir marre de*

to feel like ['fil 'laïk], *avoir envie de*

to be fond of ['fond ᵉᵘv], *aimer beaucou*p

to hike ['Haïk], *faire de la randonnée*

to be interested in ['intrᵉᵘstid in], *être intéressé par*

to iron ['aïᵉᵘn], *repasser*

to be keen on ['kin on], *être passionné de*

to knit ['nit], *tricoter*

to learn ['leun], *apprendre*

leisure park ['lèjᵉᵘr pâk], *parc de loisirs*

to like ['laïk], *bien aimer*

to love ['leuv], *aimer*

mountain biking ['ma-ountin baïking], *VTT*

paintball ['pèïntbôl], *paintball*

pottery ['potᵉᵘri], *poterie*

a ride ['raïd], *un tour*

scubadiving ['skoubᵉᵘdaïving], *plongée*

to sculpt ['skeulpt], *sculpter*

to take the bin out ['tèïk DHᵉᵘ 'bin a-out], *sortir la poubelle*

yoga ['ioᵉᵘougᵉᵘ], *yoga*

---

17 Construis des gérondifs à partir des éléments suivants pour former des noms d'activités.

1. L'escalade ....

2. La collection de monnaie ....

3. L'observation ornithologique ....

4. La course de karting ....

5. Le patin à glace ....

Noms	Verbes
bird ['beud], *oiseau*	**to climb** ['klaïm], *grimper*
coin ['koïn], *pièce de monnaie*	**to collect** ['kᵉᵘ'lèkt], *collectionner*
ice ['aïs], *glace*	**to race** ['rèïs], *piloter*
kart ['kât], *un karting (voiture)*	**to skate** ['skèït], *faire du roller/patin*
rock ['reuk], *pierre*	**to watch** ['ouôtch], *regarder*

18 Dis ce que Nathan aime ou n'aime pas faire dans la maison à partir des éléments fournis, puis complète la phrase **4** et exprime une préférence en **5**.

1. mind – not ....   **2.** hate ....   **3.** enjoy ....

....

→ OUT

4. What is his favourite chore (tâche ménagère)? .... is his favourite house chore.

5. Dust < iron : he ....

19 Théo s'ennuie. Remets les lettres dans l'ordre pour obtenir une activité, puis pose la question permettant de la lui suggérer.

1. GNIGINS NI A CROHI..

2. GLIPAYN SRUMD NI A DANB ....

3. NANIRLEG LOCEL ....

20 Relie chaque début de phrase à la suite qui lui correspond et écris le gérondif correspondant à l'illustration dans la colonne de droite.

1. She is keen ...	• •	**a.** to	....	a.
2. He's crazy ...	• •	**b.** ... on	....	b.
3. He's afraid ...	• •	**c.** like	camping...........	c.
4. She prefers hiking ...	• •	**d.** ... in	....	d.
5. She feels ...	• •	**e.** ... of	....	e.
6. He's interested ...	• •	**f.** ... with	....	f.
7. I can't ...	• •	**g.** ... about	....	g.
8. We're fed up	• •	**h.** ... bear	....	h.

21 Reformule ces énoncés à l'aide d'un gérondif sujet.

1. He wants to wear a tie. It is a good idea → ....

2. She doesn't share her snack. It is not nice → ....

Le present perfect (1/2)

Ce temps permet d'exprimer deux types d'actions :

- celles qui ont toujours cours dans le présent et que l'on traduit par un présent en français (cas qui nous intéresse ici),

- celles dont les conséquences sont importantes dans le présent (traduit par un passé composé en français). Nous verrons ce cas de figure dans l'unité 3.

Il existe une forme simple et une forme en **-ing** du present perfect.

• **Present perfect simple**

- Formation : **have** conjugué + **p.p.** (figure dans la 3ᵉ colonne des verbes irréguliers, p. 121).

FA : **I have known…**

FI : **Has she known…?**

FN : **They haven't known…**

- Utilisation : pour une action commencée dans le passé et qui continue dans le présent.

Ex. : **I have known her for two years,** *Je la connais depuis deux ans.*

• **Present perfect -ing**

- Formation : **have** conjugué + **been** + BV **-ing.**

FA : **I have been living…**

FI : **Has she been living…?**

FN : **They haven't been living…**

- Utilisation : pour une action commencée dans le passé et qui continue dans le présent, quand on veut insister sur la durée de l'action ou sur l'activité elle-même.

Ex. : **I have been living in London for 10 years,** *J'habite à Londres depuis 10 ans.*

Avec cette forme, on utilise beaucoup l'adverbe **lately,** qui signifie *dernièrement.*

Ex. : **I have been working a lot lately,** *Je travaille beaucoup dernièrement.*

On emploie également cette forme lorsque les conséquences sont visibles.

Ex. : **You've been smoking too much (lately), your teeth are getting yellow,** *Tu fumes trop (dernièrement), tes dents jaunissent.*

- **NB** : On traduit *depuis* par **for** devant une durée et par **since** devant une date ou un événement qui marque le point de départ d'une action.

Ex. : **I have known her for two years, I have known her since 2015 / since my divorce.**

How long sert à interroger sur la durée d'une action.

Ex. : **How long have you been married?** *Depuis combien de temps es-tu marié ?*

22 Corrige les erreurs éventuelles.

1. My neighbour has had dreadlocks since three weeks.

....

2. I have played the cello for 2005.

....

3. How long has your mother be a nurse?

....

4. I have always spend my holidays abroad.

....

5. I have been waited for you for two hours!

....

23 Conjugue les verbes au temps qui convient (present perfect simple ou continu).

1. My neighbour .... (be divorced) for ten years.

2. We .... (clean) the house for a long time now. Let's take a break!

3. I .... (wait) for you for an hour!

4. How long ....you .... (play) the cello? For ten years.

5. She .... (eat) too much lately, she is getting fat.

6. They .... (see) a doctor twice a month since 2015.

24 Complète les phrases avec **for** ou **since**.

1. He's had asthma .... the age of five.

2. We've had this car .... more than ten years now.

3. He has stopped shaving .... his divorce.

4. She has been working for them .... a decade.

5. The baby has been sleeping .... ˙2 o'clock.

25 Remets les mots dans le bon ordre pour obtenir une phrase correcte au present perfect progressif. Puis attribue à chacune d'elles l'énoncé exprimant la conséquence qui lui convient. Enfin, propose une traduction.

a. We're out of breath* **b.** There are books everywhere. **c.** For two hours! They're so angry!

1. lot/studying/Anna/lately/been/a/has ....

....

2. hour/been/have/for/running/an/we ....

....

3. been/ ?/they/have/long/arguing/how ....

....

*essoufflés

26 Traduis les phrases suivantes.

1. Est-ce que tu connais le beau-père de Simon ? Que fait-il dans la vie ?

....

2. Elle utilise toujours ma console de jeux !

....

3. Je m'endors toujours à minuit.

....

4. Ton voisin est faible depuis son accident.

....

5. Depuis combien de temps écris-tu un journal intime ?

....

6. Nous prenons rarement le métro.

....

7 – Vous le prenez tous les combien ?

....

– Deux fois par mois.

....

8. Mrs Sanders ne porte quasiment jamais de bijoux mais aujourd'hui elle porte un collier.

....

9. – Que fait ta sœur ?

....

– Elle est en train de jouer du violoncelle.

....

10. Mes parents sont mariés depuis 20 ans.

....

11. L'air contient de l'oxygène.

....

12. Je dors beaucoup dernièrement.

....

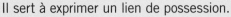

Le génitif

Il sert à exprimer un lien de possession.

- Il se construit de cette manière : possesseur + **'s** + chose « possédée ».

  Ex. : **the child's toy,** *le jouet de l'enfant*

- Pour les possesseurs singuliers se terminant par **-s** : on ajoute **'s**.

  Ex. : **Rufus's hair,** *les cheveux de Rufus*

- Pour les noms pluriels se terminant par un **s** : on ajoute juste **'**.

  Ex. : **my friends' house,** *la maison de mes amis*

- Pour les pluriels irréguliers ne se terminant pas par **s** : on ajoute **'s**.

  Ex. : **my feet's toes,** *mes doigts de pieds*

- Quand il existe plusieurs possesseurs pour un « bien » commun, le **'s** porte sur le dernier possesseur.

  Ex. : **John and Tina's baby,** *le bébé de John et de Tina*

- **NB** : on utilise aussi **'s** pour dire *chez quelqu'un.*

  Ex. : **to go to the doctor's, baker's, hairdresser's,** *aller chez le médecin, le boulanger, le coiffeur.* **I'm at Ian's,** *Je suis chez Ian.*

27 Dans chaque phrase, place le génitif de possession correct.

1. The customers…… rights.

2. There's a magazine called *Men……
Health.*

3. Karim…… and Nora…… fathers are brothers.

4. Sarah needs a new haircut. She's going to the hairdresser……

5. Oliver…… family is rich.

6. The cat is eating our mice…… cheese.

7. He's marrying the neighbours…… daughter.

8. I need some meat. Go to the butcher…… for me.

9. Helen …… and Gabriel…… mother is Mrs Herbert.

10. Is it James…… fault?

Les pronoms et adjectifs possessifs

Ils sont invariables en genre et en nombre.

Ex. : **their mother,** *leur mère,* **their children,** *leurs enfants*

Pronoms personnels sujets	I	you	he/she/it	we	you	they
Pronoms possessifs	my	your	his/her/its	our	your	their
Adjectifs possessifs	mine	yours	his/hers/Ø	ours	yours	theirs

28 Remplace l'indicateur de possession souligné par l'adjectif ou le pronom possessif qui convient.

1. This is not <u>Tina's</u> book. It's <u>our book</u>. ....

2. <u>Ian and David's</u> house is huge. <u>Your house</u> is not. ....

3. James is <u>my</u> friend : He's a friend of ....

29 Reformule à l'aide des mots suivants et d'un adjectif/pronom possessif.

to belong to ['bilong t^{eu}], *appartenir à* – **owner** ['^{eu}oun^{eur}], *propriétaire*

1. It's Helena's car. It's ...., not mine. The car .... to her.

2. Who's the .... of that house? Yann is. It's .... house.

Décrire à l'aide des adjectifs

- Tu sais déjà que les adjectifs sont invariables en anglais et que, comme en français, on peut les employer comme attributs ou épithètes (avec ou sans l'intermédiaire d'un verbe d'état comme **to be**.) Ex. : **I'm young / I'm a young woman, These men are angry / They are angry men.**

- Pour décrire quelqu'un ou quelque chose, on peut utiliser le verbe **to look** au présent simple, suivi d'un adjectif. Ex. : **He looks tired,** *Il a l'air fatigué.*
- Pour demander de quoi quelqu'un /quelque chose a l'air, on dira **what does / do** + sujet + **look like?** Ex. : **What does her sister look like?** *Comment est sa sœur ?*

Banque de mots

alive [^{eu}'laïv], *vivant*

bald [bôld], *chauve*

dead [dèd], *mort*

divorced [di'vôst], *divorcé(e)*

grandparents ['granpèr^{eu}nts], *grands-parents*

to grow ['gr^{eu}ou]/**get** ['gèt] **old**, *vieillir*

half-brother ['Hâf]/**sister**, *demi-frère/sœur*

husband ['Heusb^{eu}nd], *mari*

to look ['louk] + adj. *avoir l'air, paraître…*

married ['marid], *marié(e)*

middle-aged ['mid^{eu}l èïdjd], *d'âge moyen*

mother/father-in-law ['lô], *beau-père, belle-mère (parents du conjoint)*

no ['n^{eu}ou], *pas de …*

not … anymore [neut … 'ènimô^r], *ne plus …*

only child ['^{eu}ounli 'tchaïld], *fille/fils unique*

single ['sing^{eu}l], *célibataire*

step-father ['stèp]/**mother**, *beau-père, belle-mère (famille recomposée)*

widow(er) ['ouid^{eu}ou^{eur}], *veuve, (veuf)*

wife ['ouaïf], *épouse*

unemployed [eun'èmploïd], *sans emploi*

30 Right or Wrong? Corrige si besoin.

	Marié(e)	Divorcé(e)	Veuf(ve)	Frère/sœur	Demi-frère/sœur	Âge	Grands-parents
Mrs Davis	non	non	oui	2	0	82	décédés
Mr Picky	non	non	non	0	0	42	décédés
Pierre	oui	non	non	1	0	22	vivants

1. Mrs Davis

a. Her husband is dead.

W / R ....

b. She is an only child.

W / R ....

c. She is middle-aged.

W / R ....

2. Mr Picky

a. He is not divorced.

W / R ....

b. He has got brothers and sisters.

W / R ....

c. His grandparents are dead.

W / R ....

d. He is a teenager.

W / R ....

3. Pierre

a. He is single.

W / R ....

b. He is an only child.

W / R ....

c. He is middle-aged.

W / R ....

31 Reformule les énoncés suivants en remplaçant les parties soulignées.

1. Rob is <u>not single anymore</u>, he's ....

2. His <u>wife is dead</u>, he's a ....

3. He's .... He's <u>unemployed</u> now.

4. Anna's got <u>no brothers and sisters</u>, she's ....

5. He's got <u>no hair</u> = he's ....

6. She's got no ...., she is <u>divorced now</u>.

7. My grandma is <u>not middle-aged anymore</u>, she's ....

8. My brother is 45 now. He's <u>not young anymore</u>, he's .... - ...... now.

Banque de mots

disabled [dis'èïb^{eu}ld], *handicapé*

fat ['fat], *gros(se)*

handsome ['Hèns^{eu}m], *beau, pour un homme*

plain ['plèïn], *au physique banal*

plump ['pleump], *enrobé(e)*

pretty ['prèti], *belle*

short ['chôt], *petit(e)*

skinny ['skini], *maigre*

slim ['slim], *mince*

tall ['tôl], *grand(e)*

thin ['THin], *très mince*

ugly ['eugli], *laid(e)*

32 Qui suis-je ? Trouve à quel personnage correspond chacune des descriptions suivantes.

	beau	laid	maigre	enrobé	grand
Jean	oui	non	non	oui	non
Julien	non	oui	oui	non	oui
Louis	oui	non	non	non	non

1. I don't look ugly. I'm neither tall nor skinny. I'm handsome and plump. I'm ....

2. I'm not plump but I don't look skinny either. I'm ....

3. I'm neither handsome nor plump but I look skinny. I'm ....

33 Trouve l'adjectif qui permet de former une phrase pertinente.

1. She's not fat but she's a bit ....

2. Your sister looks too slim, she's ....

3. Mrs Oran is neither .... nor .... She looks plain.

Décrire la personnalité

cheerful ['tchif^{eu}l], *gai*

clumsy ['kleumzi], *maladroit*

funny ['feuni], *drôle*

grumpy ['greumpi], *grincheux*

helpful ['Hèlpf^{eu}l], *serviable*

lazy ['lèïzi], *paresseux*

quiet ['kouaï^{eu}t], *calme*

selfish ['sèlfich], *égoïste*

shy ['chaï], *timide*

thoughtful ['THôtf^{eu}l], *réfléchi*

34 Paula a 3 frères. Elle énumère leurs caractéristiques morales.
Attribue les adjectifs de personnalité (voir Banque de mots en page précédente)
qui conviennent à chacun d'eux en t'appuyant sur ce qu'elle nous en dit
(précise le numéro de phrase qui t'a permis de trouver entre parenthèses).

1. Eric always breaks and drops things.

2. Simon likes to tell jokes.

3. Tommy hates sharing his things.

4. Simon generally helps other people.

5. Eric complains all the time.

6. Tommy doesn't like to work.

7. Simon is often calm.

8. Eric thinks a lot before acting.

9. Tommy is usually scared of other people.

10. Simon is always happy.

Eric is/looks: .... ( ), ... ( ),
and .... ( )

Simon is/looks: .... ( ), ... ( ),
.... ( ), and .... ( )

Tommy is/looks: .... ( ), ... ( ),
and .... ( )

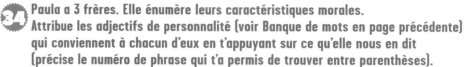

Banque de mots

Décrire un endroit

cluttered ['kleut^{eu}d], *encombré*

cosy ['k^{eu}ouzi], *confortable, douillet*

cramped ['krampt], *très petit*

dirty ['deuti], *sale*

dusty ['deusti], *poussiéreux*

filthy ['filTHi], *crasseux*

fussy ['feusi], *tatillon*

messy ['mèsi], *en désordre*

neat and tidy ['nit ^{eu}n 'taïdi], *propre, net*

shabby (meuble) ['chabi], *usé, miteux*

spacious ['spèïch^{eu}s], *spacieux*

35 Remets les lettres dans l'ordre.

1. Peter, go tidy and clean your bedroom, it's
SEMYS .... and HYTLIF .... in there!

2. Our sofa looks old and BASHYB ....
We need to buy a new one.

3. I wash the YTIRD .... laundry on Sundays.

4. I have accumulated things for 10 years, our house
is CRELTUTED ....

5. Anna has allergies. She is coughing because the room
is STUDY ....!

6. My mother is fussy. She always wants things to be
TENA DAN DITY ....

7. Their flat is not spacious at all. It's even a bit
PREDMAC .... but it's SOYC ....
You feel good in it.

Adjectifs particuliers

Les adjectifs **afraid, alive, alone, asleep, ill, awake** ne peuvent s'employer que comme attributs. Ex. : **this child is alone / this is ~~an alone child~~ ; the baby is asleep / don't wake up ~~an asleep baby~~**. Pour exprimer la même idée, il faut employer un adjectif différent.

Adjectifs ne s'employant pas comme épithètes	Adjectifs à utiliser à la place
afraid	**scared** ou **frightened** *(effrayé)*
asleep	**sleeping** *(endormi)*
ill	**sick** *(malade)*
alive	**living** *(vivant)*
alone	**lonely** *(seul)*

 Place les adjectifs à l'endroit qui convient dans chaque phrase.

1. alone/lonely | My friend Zack is always .... He's a(n) .... boy.

2. sick/ill | This man is as ...... as Mr Tomson, who is a very ...... man.

3. afraid/scared | I don't know any .... dogs. My dog is never ....

4. alive/living | He's the last victim .... = he's the last .... victim.

Les adjectifs employés comme noms

- Ils désignent un ensemble et ne prennent pas de **-s**. Ex. : **the young,** *les jeunes* ; **the blind,** *les aveugles* ; **the sick,** *les malades* ; **the living,** *les vivants* ; **the dead,** *les morts,* **the unemployed,** *les sans-emploi*

- Ils restent au singulier mais le verbe qui les suit est au pluriel. Ex. : **The rich generally have fancy cars,** *Les riches ont généralement des voitures de luxe*

- Si tu souhaites individualiser, il faudra que tu ajoutes un nom. Ex. : **a blind man,** *un aveugle*

Adjectifs de nationalité

- singulier
  a Frenchman, *un Français*
  an Englishman, *un Anglais*
  a Pole, *un Polonais*
  a Spaniard, *un Espagnol*
  a Chinese man, *un Chinois*
  a German, an American, *un Allemand, un Américain*

- pluriel
  the French, *les Français*
  the English, *les Anglais*
  the Polish, *les Polonais*
  the Spanish, *les Espagnols*
  the Chinese, *les Chinois*
  the Germans, Americans, *les Allemands, les Américains*

NB : Seuls les adjectifs de nationalité en **-an** prennent un **s** au pluriel.

37 Place chacun des deux éléments fournis entre parenthèses à l'endroit qui convient dans chaque phrase.

1. .... always lives in the memory of .... (the living / a dead man)

2. Our neighbour is a .... are hardworking people. (Pole / The Polish)

3. .... have less money than .... (Young men / the retired*)

4. .... are composed of .... (Frenchmen / the French)

5. Her husband is .... are very cheerful. (The Irish / an Irishman)

6. The .... love cooking seafood. My husband is a .... (Spanish / Spaniard)

*retraités

Les adjectifs en *-ing* et en *-ed*

Les adjectifs se terminant en **-ing** indiquent la source d'une émotion, alors que ceux en **-ed** indiquent le ressenti qui en découle.

Ex. : **this is boring → I am bored; this is surprising → I am surprised**

38 Entoure l'adjectif qui convient.

1. My little sister is *frightened/frightening* of spiders.

2. What an *amazing/amazed* film, I love it!

3. Tom's friend is *annoyed/annoying*, I don't like him.

4. I'm *annoying/annoyed* because he doesn't want to help me.

5. This horror film is really *frightened/frightening*!

6. Wow, you can play the cello and the drums?! I'm *amazing/amazed*!

Banque de mots

to amaze [ᵉᵘ'mèïz], *étonner, épater*
to annoy [ᵉᵘ'noï], *énerver*
famous ['fèïmᵉᵘs], *célèbre*
fashion ['fachᵉᵘn], *mode*
to frighten ['fraïtᵉᵘn], *faire peur, effrayer*
hand ['Hand], *main*
homesick ['Hᵉᵘoumsik], *qui a le mal du pays*
huge ['Hioudj], *énorme*
magnificent [mag'nifisᵉᵘnt], *magnifique*
medieval [mèdi'ivᵉᵘl], *médiéval*
mind ['maïnd], *esprit*
to miss ['mis], *éprouver le manque de*
narrow ['narᵉᵘou], *étroit*
open ['ᵉᵘoupᵉᵘn], *ouvert*
shape ['chèïp], *forme*
way ['ouèï], *manière*

Les adjectifs composés

- Ce sont des adjectifs formés de deux mots, le premier venant apporter une précision sur le deuxième.

  Ex. : **a green-eyed woman,** *une femme aux yeux verts* ; **a well-paid job,** *un emploi bien payé*

- Il existe diverses combinaisons possibles, dont nom + p.p. (ex. : **home-made,** *fait maison*), adj. + nom + **-ed** (**brown-haired**),

  nom ou adj. + **-ing** (ex. : **good-looking,** *beau*), etc.

- Comme tous les adjectifs, ils sont invariables. Attention donc aux erreurs car certains adjectifs composés peuvent comporter des chiffres.

  Ex. : *un livre de 200 pages,* **a two-hundred page book**, pas de **-s** à *page* !

 Forme des adjectifs composés en reliant chaque élément de gauche à un élément de droite en A et complète les phrases fournies en B (qui pourront d'ailleurs te servir d'indices).

A.

1. well-	•	•	**a.** handed
2. home	•	•	**b.** minded
3. life-	•	•	**c.** haired
4. animal	•	•	**d.** time
5. left-	•	•	**e.** known
6. open-	•	•	**f.** old
7. part	•	•	**g.** changing
8. old-	•	•	**h.** fashioned
9. long-	•	•	**i.** sick
10. two-year	•	•	**j.** shaped

B.

1. Children love ………-shaped biscuits.

2. I'm tolerant = I don't have a narrow mind = I'm open-………

3. It modifies the way you do or see things = it's a …………-changing experience.

4. If your grandparents don't have modern ways, they are ………-fashioned.

5. When you miss your country/town/family, you're ………sick.

6. Someone famous is very well-………

7. My sister doesn't have short hair, she is a ………-……… girl.

8. Sam is a little child, he's a ………-……… …………… boy.

9. I don't use my right hand to do things, I'm ………-………

10. When you don't work all the time, you have a ………-……… job.

L'ordre des adjectifs

Voici une règle à retenir pour ne plus t'embrouiller : plus l'adjectif est subjectif (jugement, avis, commentaire) et plus il est éloigné du nom. Tu ordonneras donc ainsi :

jugement/avis – taille – âge – couleur – nationalité – nom. Ex. : **a boring old Irish teacher**

40 Forme des descriptions correctes à partir des éléments suivants (les noms donnés en images et les adjectifs à remettre dans l'ordre).

1. Sam is a ....

....

(German
– small
– ugly –
brown)

2. This is a ....

....

(medieval – huge – Scottish
– magnificent)

3. Mr Sanchez is a

....

....

....

(ninety-year-old –
tall – Spanish – old-
fashioned)

Les noms composés

- Ils sont formés de deux mots, le premier apportant une précision sur le deuxième (fonction, type, matière, nature, etc.).
- Les combinaisons les plus fréquentes sont : nom + nom (ex. : **toothpaste,** *dentifrice*), adj. + verbe (ex. : **frying pan,** *poêle à frire*), adj. + nom (ex. : **hotdog**), verbe + nom (ex. : **driving licence,** *permis de conduire*).
- Seul le deuxième nom peut porter la marque du pluriel.

Ex. : **hotdogs, driving licences, toothpastes**

41 Relie un élément de la colonne de gauche à un de la colonne de droite pour construire des reformulations pertinentes.

1. You can cook your sausages in it = it's a **frying**	•	•	**hole** *(trou)*
2. Henry talks all the time. He is a **chatter**	•	•	**work** *(travail)*
3. Sandy has got red hair. She is a **red**	•	•	**cut** *(coupe)*
4. I don't like vanilla **ice**	•	•	**pan**
5. Dusting and ironing are part of the **house**	•	•	**head**
6. He's so noisy! He's looking through the **key**	•	•	**box** *(boîte)*
7. You hair is too long, you need a **hair**	•	•	**cream** *(crème)*

Déduis-en comment on traduit les mots suivants.

a. trou de serrure ....

b. pipelette ....

c. rouquine... .

d. glace ....

e. tâches ménagères ....

f. coupe de cheveux ....

Banque de mots

book case ['boukèïs], *bibliothèque*

case ['kèïs], *boîte, étui (par extension endroit où l'on range des choses)*

to clean ['klin], *nettoyer, faire le ménage*

pill ['pil], *pilule*

to put ['pout], *mettre*

to shave ['chèïv], *se raser*

stick ['stik], *bâton, bout de bois*

vending machine ['vènding m^{eu} 'chin], *distributeur*

wall [ouôl], *mur*

 Place les mots suivants dans les espaces correspondants pour former des phrases pertinentes.

pill – shaving – paper – cleaning

1. The living room looks old and shabby. We've had the same wall .... for 20 years.

2. My mother does not sleep well and she sometimes takes sleeping .... (s).

3. My father has got a beard so he never uses .... cream.

4. The .... lady comes at home once a week. She hoovers the floor.

machine – stick – pool – case

5. Our grandmother is very old. She needs a walking .... now.

6. I go to the swimming .... twice a month.

7. Vending .... (s) usually contain a lot of junk food.

8. There are many English novels in my book ....

La forme exclamative

Il existe deux grands types de phrases exclamatives :

• **What a(n) / Ø** + nom et **such a(n) / Ø** + nom ; l'exclamation porte sur un nom. Ex. : **What a nice boy!** ; **What a nice house she's got!**

She's got such a nice house! ; **They're such nice boys!**

• **So** + adj. (ou adv.) et **how** + adj. (ou adv.) ; l'exclamation porte sur un adverbe ou un adjectif.

Ex. : **How funny this man is!*** ; **They've got so much money!**

*Attention à l'ordre des mots ! À ne pas confondre avec la forme interrogative **How funny is this man?**

43 Relie les éléments pour former des phrases correctes.

1. What an	•	•	**a.** friends!
2. How interesting this	•	•	**b.** annoying man!
3. Your necklace is	•	•	**c.** beautiful necklace!
4. What helpful	•	•	**d.** novel is!
5. How interesting is	•	•	**e.** so beautiful!
6. This is such a	•	•	**f.** this novel?

44 Forme une phrase exclamative correcte en utilisant les éléments fournis.

1. what – pasta – disgusting ....

....

2. how – that room – cosy...

....

3. such – your father – good-looking...........................

....

4. how – They've got cute freckles ....

....

5. so – these strawberries – sweet ....

....

6. what – he's wearing a cool hoodie......

....

....

Les articles, suite

Nous avons commencé à aborder les articles et déterminants en début d'unité avec les noms. Creusons un peu en faisant quelques rappels que tu aurais pu oublier. On utilise :

- **Ø** : devant les noms indénombrables ou les pluriels (ex. : **I love Ø rice / Ø cats**), devant les titres officiels (ex. : **President Ø Clinton**), les noms de pays (ex. : **Ø Germany is bigger than France**) sauf <u>the</u> **USA,** et les sports (ex. : **my father plays Ø rugby**).

- **the** : devant des noms quand on parle d'un exemple en particulier (ex. : **the cat is out,** *le chat est dehors.* On sait de quel chat on parle, c'est notre chat), les éléments faisant partie de l'univers commun (ex. : **the sky ; the wind,** *le vent*) et les instruments de musique (ex. : **I play the guitar**).

- **a/an** : dans certaines phrases exclamatives, devant les professions (ex. : **his mother is a teacher**) et dans certaines expressions courantes à connaître (ex. : **to have a fever / headache,** *avoir de la fièvre / mal à la tête* ; **to make a noise,** *faire du bruit*).

45 Complète les espaces par **a, an, the** ou **Ø**.

1. I love visiting ...... United States but my parents prefer ...... Italy.

2. My father is always watching ...... films about ...... Second World War.

3. My brother is ...... fireman. I'd like to become ...... astronaut.

4. ...... koalas and ...... kangaroos live in ...... Australia.

5. You're such ...... idiot! Stop making ...... noise, I've got ...... headache!

6. My sisters play ...... cello. I prefer to play ...... handball.

7. ...... English people play ...... cricket.

8. This is such ...... delicious piece of chocolate!

9. I generally don't like ...... coffee but ...... coffee we're drinking now is not bad.

10. I no longer drink ...... milk. It makes me sick.

11. ...... Queen Victoria was ...... famous English queen.

Bravo, tu es venu à bout de la première unité ! Il est maintenant temps de comptabiliser les icônes et de reporter le résultat en page 128 pour l'évaluation finale.

Unité 2
Exprimer des situations futures et virtuelles et les différents types de modalité

Le futur

	Formation	Utilisation
be about to	**to be** + **about to** + BV Ex. : **we are about to eat, is she about to eat?, they're not about to eat**	Pour dire *être sur le point de*
be going to	**to be** + **going to** + BV Ex. : **they are going to run, is she going to run?, you're not going to run**	Action prévue dans un futur proche ou déductible à partir des circonstances. Ex. : **she's taking a book, she's going to read**
présent -ing	Tu sais le faire !	Décision prise et organisée ; on mentionne d'ailleurs souvent une date, une heure, un jour. Ex. : **I'm seeing Robert tomorrow**, *Je vois Robert demain*
présent simple	Tu sais le faire !	Événement, horaire planifié par un agent extérieur. Ex. : **My father retires next year**, *Mon père part en retraite l'année prochaine*
will	FA : **I /.../ they + will + BV** Ex. : **Ok, we will go on a picnic!** FI : **Will + I /.../ they + BV?** Ex. : **Will she go on a picnic?** FN : **I /.../ they + will not (won't) + BV** Ex. : **They won't come at 6**	- Intention avec idée de volonté sous-jacente, - Décision prise au moment où on l'énonce, - Action sous condition. Ex. : **We'll go on a picnic if it doesn't rain**, *Nous irons pique-niquer s'il ne pleut pas*
will be + ing	FA : **I /.../ they + will be + BV -ing** FI : **will + I /.../ they + BV -ing?** FN : **I /.../ they + will not + BV -ing**	Projection dans le futur d'une action qui sera en cours de réalisation à un moment du futur envisagé. Ex. : **Tomorrow, we will be running New York's marathon**, *Demain, nous serons en train de courir le marathon de New York*

Banque de mots

abroad [ᵉᵘ'brᵉᵘoud], *à l'étranger*

to apologise [ᵉᵘ'polodjaïz], *s'excuser*

to come back ['keum 'bak], *revenir*

to die ['daï], *mourir*

to dump ['deump] **someone**, *rompre avec quelqu'un*

engaged ['èngèïdjd], *fiancé*

factory ['faktri], *usine*

to forgive [fᵉᵘ'giv], *pardonner*

Greece ['Gris], *Grèce*

to intend to [in'tènd tᵉᵘ], *avoir l'intention de*

lawyer ['loïᵉᵘr], *avocat*

to leave ['liv], *partir, quitter*

to lend ['lènd], *prêter*

next ['nèkst] **week, month, year**, *la semaine, le mois, l'année prochain(e)*

to be over [bi 'ᵉᵘouvᵉᵘr], *être terminé*

to plan ['plan], *prévoir de*

pregnant ['prègnᵉᵘnt], *enceinte*

to propose [prᵉᵘ 'pᵉᵘouz], *demander en mariage*

to quit ['kouit], *démissionner*

to recover [ri'keuvᵉᵘr], *se remettre*

to save ['sèïv], *économiser*

soon ['soun], *bientôt*

sore throat ['sô THrᵉᵘout], *mal de gorge*

to swim ['souim], *nager*

tomorrow [tᵉᵘ'morᵉᵘou], *demain*

to yawn ['iôn], *bâiller*

1 Associe chaque début d'énoncé à la construction verbale qui convient.

1. I'm ◯ **2.** I'm going ◯ **3.** I am about ◯ **4.** I will ◯ **5.** I will be ◯

a. to leave the country **b.** leaving the country **c.** leave the country

2 Remets les éléments dans l'ordre et indique auxquels des contextes futurs listés en dessous correspondent les phrases ainsi formées.

1. a better job/I will buy/when/a new car/I get

5. the/factory/tomorrow/visits/president/our

2. dinner/we/about/are/start/to

6. – I'm going to the cinema tonight.

3. girfriend/dumping/his/Eric/is/tonight

– you/come/I'll/with !

4. some/will/money/you/I/lend

7. to/sad/she/cry/very/going/looks/she's

a. action sous condition
b. déduction à partir des circonstances
c. événement planifié par un agent extérieur
d. décision prise et organisée
e. événement imminent
f. décision prise au moment où on l'énonce
g. volonté

3 Construis des phrases pertinentes au futur, comme dans l'exemple.
Dans les phrases 4-5, la tâche est plus rude, car il te faudra aussi trouver un adjectif ou un verbe manquant. Enfin, reformule la phrase 6.

It/cold : snow → It's cold, it's going to snow.

1. Samuel/sick : but - not die → ....

2. Anna/yawning : fall asleep → ....

3. My father/take his razor : shave → ....

4. Clara/............ : have a baby ....

5. Ian and Sofia/............ : get married ....

6. .... = you are going to say "sorry".

4 Entoure la forme de futur qui convient.

1. The concert begins – is beginning at 10 pm.

2. I am making - will make pasta when you are - will be hungry.

3. Hurry up, the bus is about to - will leave.

4. Give me the phone. I'm going to call - will be calling Paul.

5. We are telling - will tell you as soon as we know more.

6. I hope you get - will get better soon.

5 Si l'on devait reformuler ces phrases avec **will** ou **be + -ing**, lequel conviendrait le mieux ?

1. Is it your plan to come to my party? ....

2. Do you wish to come to my party? ....

3. Do you intend to come to my party? ....

4. Do you feel like coming to my party? ....

6 Complète les phrases avec le présent **-ing** ou **will**.

1. I .... (forgive) you if you apologise.

2. Ian .... (propose) to Rachel tomorrow.

3. John .... (quit) his job next week.

4. She .... (help) you when you're nicer to her.

5. – Someone's knocking at the door.
– I ...... (get) it!

7 Que seront-ils en train de faire au moment futur précisé ?

1. Tomorrow → I drive my new ....

2. When you visit me in a month → I live in my new ....

3. This time next week → we run the marathon ....

8 Pose les questions portant sur les parties soulignées.

1. The Shakespeare play begins <u>at eight</u>.

....

2. We're going to live abroad <u>for a couple of years</u>.

....

3. I will not sing because <u>I have got a sore throat</u>.

....

4. Tomorrow <u>she</u>'ll be working with us.

....

9 Traduis les phrases suivantes.

1. J'espère que tu te remettras bientôt.

....

2. J'achèterai un nouvel ordinateur si nous économisons suffisamment.

....

3. Je ne passerai pas l'aspirateur (*pas envie*).

....

4. Quand je serai grand, je serai avocat.

....

5. Est-ce que le film commence à 21 heures ?

....

6. Dans une semaine, tu seras en train de nager en Grèce.

....

Can, be able to et may

	Formation	Utilisation
can [kan]	Se conjugue de la même façon à toutes les personnes. Ex. : **FA** : I /.../ they can swim **FI** : Can I /.../ they swim? **FN** : I /.../ they cannot (can't [kãt]) swim 	Ne s'utilise qu'au présent. **FA, FI** : - capacité Ex. : **She can speak Russian** - autorisation Ex. : **Can I invite my friend?** - valeur de probabilité : possibilité ex. : **Dogs can bite sometimes** **FN** : - incapacité - absence d'autorisation - valeur de probabilité : impossibilité Ex. : **You can't be serious!** Avec les verbes de perception : Ex. : **I can hear a train**
be able to	**Be able to** + BV. On conjugue **to be**, le reste ne change pas. Ex. : **FA** : **She is able to help you** **FI** : **Will they be able to help you?** **FN** : **They won't be able to help you**	S'utilise à tous les temps. **FA, FI** : capacité **FN** : incapacité Contrairement à **can** qui indique une capacité permanente, **be able to** relève davantage d'une capacité ponctuelle.
be allowed to	**Be allowed to** + BV. On conjugue **to be**, le reste ne change pas. Ex. : **FA** : **She is allowed to help you** **FI** : **Will they be allowed to help you?** **FN** : **They won't be allowed to help you**	S'utilise à tous les temps. **FA, FI** : autorisation, permission **FN** : interdiction

10 Relie chaque mot à sa définition (la plupart des termes de reformulation sont transparents afin que tu n'aies pas trop de mal !).

1. to introduce	●	●	**a.** not late or early
2. to cancel	●	●	**b.** meeting
3. to lie	●	●	**c.** to speak very loudly
4. on time	●	●	**d.** was hoping better
5. compulsory	●	●	**e.** not polite
6. appointment	●	●	**f.** regulation
7. disappointed	●	●	**g.** to annul
8. to shout	●	●	**h.** obligatory
9. rule	●	●	**i.** to cut with your teeth
10. to bite	●	●	**j.** not to tell the truth
11. rude	●	●	**k.** to present to someone

11 Entoure, pour chaque proposition, la seule structure grammaticalement correcte.

1. They can't → **a.** seeing anyone **b.** to see anyone **c.** see anyone

2. He will have → **a.** tell me **b.** telling me **c.** to tell me

3. You → **a.** not may smoke **b.** may not smoke **c.** may not smoking

4. a. Has she to help you? **b.** Does she have to help you? **c.** Does she have helping you?

5. I won't be able → **a.** to help you **b.** helping you **c.** help you

12 Complète les reformulations suivantes.

1. Louis cannot walk anymore, he's ....

2. Louisa ...., she's deaf.

3. My uncle Bob .... , he's blind.

4. Are you .... ? Can't you speak?

13 **Entoure l'expression qui convient le mieux et donne une traduction des phrases que tu auras formées.**

1. I can't *stand – help – get* people who are always late.

....

2. My brother can't *wait – help – stand* biting his nails.

....

3. She's so lazy. She can't even *help – wait – be bothered* to answer the phone.

....

4. They're so happy. They can't *wait – help – stand – be bothered to* see you next week.

....

5. I can't *get – help – stand* enough of pasta. I eat some almost every day.

....

Banque de mots

to allow [ᵉᵘ'lao], *autoriser à*

to be allowed [ᵉᵘ'la-oud] **to**, *avoir la permission de*

appointment [ᵉᵘ'poïntmᵉᵘnt], *rendez-vous*

to bite ['baït], *ronger, mordre*

to borrow ['borᵉᵘou], *emprunter*

to cancel ['kansᵉᵘl], *annuler*

compulsory [kᵉᵘm'peulsori], *obligatoire*

depressed [di'prèst], *déprimé*

disappointed [disᵉᵘ'poïntid], *déçu*

to go on a diet ['daïᵉᵘt], *être au régime*

to introduce [intrᵉᵘ'dious] **to**, *présenter à*

law ['lô], *loi*

to lie ['laï], *mentir*

nail ['nèïl], *ongle*

on time [on 'taïm], *à l'heure*

to pass an exam ['pas ᵉᵘn ig'zam], *réussir un examen*

to rent ['rènt], *louer*

rude ['roud], *grossier*

rule ['roul], *règle*

to save money ['sèïv 'meuni], *économiser de l'argent*

to shout ['chaout], *crier*

to solve ['solv], *résoudre*

subtitles ['seubtaïtᵉᵘlz], *sous-titres*

to tend to ['tènd], *avoir tendance à*

truth ['trouTH], *vérité*

Expressions avec *can't*

I can't bear + nom ou **to** + BV / **I can't stand** + **-ing**, *je ne supporte pas…*

I can't be bothered to, *j'ai la flemme de…*

I can't get enough of, *j'adore, je ne me lasse pas de…*

I can't help + **ing**, *je ne peux pas m'empêcher de…*

I can't wait to, *je suis impatient de…*

Must et have to

	Formation	Utilisation
must [meust]	Se conjugue de la même façon à toutes les personnes. Ex. : **FA** : I /.../ they must work more **FI** : Must I /.../ they work more? **FN** : I /.../ they mustn't [meus^{eu}nt] work more	Ne s'utilise qu'au présent. FA, FI : - obligation - valeur de probabilité : probabilité forte **FN** : interdiction
have to	**Have** conjugué + **to** + BV. Ex. : **FA** : he has to / will have to work more **FI** : do/will they have to work more? **FN** : I /.../ they don't/won't have to work more	S'utilise à tous les temps. FA, FI : obligation FN : absence d'obligation

14 Détache les mots au bon endroit pour former des phrases correctes, puis indique quelle(s) phrase(s) correspond(ent) à... (attention, toutes les phrases ne correspondent pas forcément à l'une des fonctions citées)

a. une interdiction _____

b. une incapacité _____

c. une absence d'obligation _____

d. une autorisation_____

e. une demande d'autorisation_____

f. une capacité _____

g. une très forte probabilité _____

h. une obligation _____

1. Myhusbandcanhaveabadtempersometimes	**9.** They'renotabletosolvethatproblem ....
2. Youmustbeverydepressed	**10.** Youcanbecomealawyerifyouworkhard ....
3. Youmustrentacheaperflat	**11.** MayIborrowyourlaptop? ....
4. Willyoubeallowedtoleaveearlier?	**12.** WintercanbeverycoldinCanada ....
5. Itcan'tbeeasyforyou	**13.** Iwillhavetotellthetruthtothepolice ....
6. Youmustn'tlie	**14.** Willtheybeabletoarriveontime? ....
7. Ican'thangaboutwithmyfriendstoday	**15.** Shecan'tcookverywell ....
8. Theydon'thavetotaketheunderground	**16.** Youmayplayvideogamesifyoudoyourhomework ....

15 Entoure la (ou les) formes modale(s) qui permet(tent) de constituer des phrases grammaticalement et logiquement correctes.

1. My wife *can't – can – must – has to* speak Spanish very well. But her English is bad.

2. I *must – don't have to – have to – can* arrive at work before 9 or my boss will fire me.

3. It *can't – mustn't – must* be hard to have two jobs.

4. I can't help you today but I *will be able to – have to – can't – must* do it tomorrow.

5. Poor Sam, it *mustn't – must – can't – doesn't have to* be easy for him.

6. You *can't – mustn't – don't have to – are not allowed to* use your phone during classes.

7. You *can – can't – have to – are able to – don't have to* cook, I'll do it.

8. Anna doesn't want to date you. You *must – can – don't have to – mustn't* be so disappointed.

9. You're too far from me. I *mustn't – can't – don't have to – can* see you.

16 Change de forme en veillant à garder le même sens modal.

1. Can you hear the neighbour sing?

(FN) ....

2. It must be getting late now.

(FN) ....

3. You don't have to call me.

(FA) ....

4. She's not able to hike long distances.

(FI) ....

5. She's allowed to run again.

(FI) ....

6. May I introduce you to my wife?

(FN)...

17 Mets les phrases suivantes au futur.

1. I can't save much money.

....

2. They must stop biting their nails.

....

3. You may not smoke in my house.

....

Différence entre *have to* et *must* au présent

Avec **have to**, l'obligation est imposée de l'extérieur (règlement, autorité, etc.) alors qu'avec **must**, le locuteur pense que c'est nécessaire et s'impose à lui-même de faire quelque chose.

18 Complète les phrases suivantes avec **have/has to** ou **must**.

1. I want to pass my exam, so I .... study every day.

2. Andreas .... go on a diet. His doctor wants it.

3. I have a cavity (*carie*), I .... go to the dentist's.

4. The rules are very clear. You .... arrive before 9 a.m.

Le cas de *need*

- **Need** est à la fois un verbe signifiant *avoir besoin de* (ex. : **She doesn't need money**) et un auxiliaire modal. Comme modal, on ne l'utilise qu'aux **FN** (**I /.../ they needn't** + BV) et **FI** (**need I /.../ they** + BV?).

- Avec **don't need to**, le locuteur énonce un fait sans jugement.

  Ex. : **You don't need eggs to make a pizza.**

- Avec **needn't**, au contraire, il exprime une absence d'obligation plus subjective.

Ex. : **You needn't bring an umbrella.** Sous-entendu : **because I think it's not going to rain.**

- À la **FI**, le modal **need** sert à demander un avis.

Ex. : **Need I bring an umbrella?** *Est-ce que tu juges nécessaire que je prenne un parapluie ?*

19 Complète les phrases suivantes avec **don't/doesn't need** ou **needn't**.

1. Lola .... subtitles, she can watch a film in original version.

2. You .... shout! I'm not deaf!

3. You .... to study law to become a policeman.

4. They .... cook, we'll go to the restaurant.

20 Pose les questions portant sur les éléments soulignés.

1. In boarding schools you have to go to bed <u>before 11</u>.

....

2. We needn't bring <u>a snack</u>.

....

3. I must help my sister <u>because she doesn't understand her lesson well</u>.

....

4. <u>Susan</u> can be rude sometimes.

....

21 Reformule les énoncés suivants en utilisant un des modaux vus précédemment.

1. She doesn't have the permission to go out.

She ....

2. They are certainly playing rugby.

They ....

3. He has the capacities to work hard.

He ....

4. Surely it's not his fault. It's not possible.

It ....

5. Get up. It is an obligation and you know it.

You ....

6. Do I take my coat? Is it necessary?

.... I .... ?

22 Traduis les phrases suivantes.

1. Pourras-tu être à l'heure ?

....

2. Tu n'as pas besoin d'annuler le rendez-vous. Je le ferai.

....

3. Je ne peux pas m'empêcher d'être déçu.

....

4. Il doit être en train de dormir.

....

5. Mon voisin est sourd et muet. Mais il voit.

....

6. Il faut respecter les règles quand on joue au rugby. C'est obligatoire.

....

7. Je dois rentrer plus tôt ce soir. Mon père a besoin de moi.

....

La suggestion et le souhait

	Formation	Utilisation
shall	**Shall we** + BV?	À la FI pour faire une suggestion. Ex. : **Shall we go to the concert?** *Veux-tu aller au concert ?*
could	**Could** + sujet + BV?	Pour une demande polie. Ex. : **Could you open the door for me, please?**
would like	FA : sujet + **would like to** + BV FI : **Would** + sujet + **like** + BV?	Pour formuler un souhait ou une proposition polie. Ex. : **I would like to be a nurse** ; **I would like an apple, please** ; **Would you like a cup of tea?**
would rather	FA : sujet + **would rather** + BV FI : **Would** + sujet + **rather** + BV FN : sujet + **would rather** + **not**	Pour exprimer une préférence dans un contexte particulier (contrairement à **to prefer**, qui exprime une préférence plus permanente). Ex. : **I generally prefer coffee but today I would rather have tea.**

Banque de mots

ashamed [^{eu}'chèïmd], *honteux*

to apologise [^{eu}'polodjaïz], *s'excuser*

to blow one's nose ['bl^{eu}ou oueunz 'n^{eu}ouz], *se moucher*

to burst into tears ['beust int^{eu} ti^{eu}z], *fondre en larmes*

careers adviser [k^{eu}'ri^{eu}z ^{eu}'dvaïz^{eur}], *conseiller d'orientation*

to chat online ['tchat 'onlaïn], *chatter en ligne*

computer programmer [k^{eu}m'pi**ou**t^{eur} pr^{eu}ougram^{eur}], *programmeur informatique*

cop ['kop], *flic (familier)*

to do the laundry ['lôndri], *faire sa lessive*

to exercise ['èks^{eu}saïz], *faire du sport*

to fail ['fèïl], *échouer*

to feel dizzy ['fil 'dizi], *avoir le tournis/vertige*

to forgive [f^{eu}'giv], *pardonner*

funeral ['fiounr^{eu}l], *enterrement*

to give a hand ['giv ^{eu} 'Hand], *donner un coup de main*

to hear some news ['Hi^{eu} s^{eu}m 'ni**ou**z], *apprendre une nouvelle*

highway code ['Haïouèï k^{eu}oud], *Code de la route*

in a good mood ['mo**ud**], *de bonne humeur*

to go on strike ['straïk], *faire grève*

junk food ['djeunk fo**ud**], *malbouffe*

to make a reservation [rèz^{eu}'vèïch^{eu}n], *réserver*

mark ['mâk], *note*

on average ['avridj], *en moyenne*

to order ['ôd^{eur}], *commander*

poor ['pô^r], *médiocre*

relieved [ri'livd], *soulagé*

report [ri'pôt], *bulletin*

to rest ['rèst], *se reposer*

return ticket [ri'te**un** tikit], *ticket aller-retour*

to run ['reun], *couler (nez)*

sales ['sèïlz], *soldes*

to share ['chè^{eur}], *partager*

to skip ['skip], *sauter, passer*

to socialize ['s^{eu}ouch^{eu}laïz], *sortir, voir des gens*

to spend money ['spènd 'meuni], *dépenser de l'argent*

starter ['stât^{eur}], *entrée (à table)*

straight-A student ['strèït èï stioud^{eu}nt], *élève qui n'a que des A*

stranger ['strèïndj^{eur}], *inconnu*

to switch off ['souitch of], *éteindre*

taxes ['taksiz], *impôts*

together [t^{eu}'gèDH^{eur}], *ensemble*

to travel ['trav^{eu}l], *voyager*

to walk the dog, ['ou**ô**k] *promener le chien*

to water ['ou**ô**t^{eur}], *arroser*

well-done ['ouèl 'deun], *bravo*

worried ['oueurid], *inquiet*

23 Verbes cachés — trouve les 10 verbes qui sont cachés dans cette grille et place-les à côté de leur traduction (essaie de mémoriser la Banque de mots avant).

1. voyager : to ....

2. partager : to ....

3. dépenser : to ....

4. commander (restaurant) : to ....

5. pardonner : to ....

6. s'excuser : to ....

7. faire du sport : to ....

8. se reposer : to ....

9. sortir, voir des gens : to ....

10. échouer : to ....

R	E	E	Z	T	I	H	E	X	P	S	D
A	E	F	M	Q	O	X	F	U	O	P	E
X	Q	S	O	G	E	E	C	C	O	E	F
E	H	O	T	R	Q	C	I	M	Z	N	A
O	S	C	C	P	G	A	L	Y	Y	D	I
E	U	I	G	F	L	I	Z	S	N	Q	L
I	S	W	G	I	W	O	V	Z	D	N	E
E	S	O	Z	O	S	M	A	E	W	E	I
D	R	E	W	N	L	T	R	A	V	E	L
O	B	A	T	F	N	O	R	D	E	R	D
U	Q	Z	H	T	C	J	P	A	H	X	U
G	H	Y	X	S	N	X	Z	A	K	N	R

24 Complète la grille suivante (les mots en anglais sont dans la Banque de mots).

Across (horiz.)

2. Cérémonie pour les morts

5. On l'est quand on dit
   « ouf, je l'ai échappé belle ! »

7. Pas seul

10. Récapitulatif écrit de tes notes

Down (vert.)

1. On l'est quand on se lève
   du bon pied : **in a good**…

3. On l'est quand on n'est
   pas fier de quelque chose

4. On l'est quand on se fait
   un sang d'encre

6. Défilé de contestation

8. Familier pour policier

9. Avant le plat principal

25 Remets les mots dans l'ordre pour obtenir des phrases pertinentes et propose une traduction.

1. computer/like/he/programmer/be/would/to/a ....

....

2. too/I/tonight/bed/rather/not/to/would/go/late ....

....

3. you/flowers/water/please/could/the/? ....

....

4. go/shall/together/to/we/party/the/? ....

....

5. to/does/to/rest/or/prefer/she/socialize/? ....

....

26 Pour chacune des propositions, écris deux phrases : une avec **would like** et une avec **would rather**.

1. I – make a reservation ....

....

2. they – travel more ....

....

3. she – buy a return ticket to Leeds? ....

....

27 Complète les phrases avec **prefer, would rather** ou **shall**.

1. If you .... apples to chocolate, ... we .... have some apple pie, then?

2. I .... my blue tie but I .... wear my black tie for the funeral.

3. I .... have my steak well-done tonight.

4. .... we .... go to the museum? Or .... you .... stay home this Friday?

5. I .... not to stay home on Fridays. .... we .... go to the pub?

28 Transforme les phrases suivantes, comme dans l'exemple.

please / you / walk the dog – I would like it
→ Could you walk the dog?

1. please / you / not smoke in the house – I would like it.

....

2. please / you / give me a hand – I would like it.

....

29 Traduis les phrases suivantes.

1. Nous aimerions passer nos vacances au Japon, et si on y allait ensemble ?

....

2. Aimeriez-vous passer commande, monsieur ?

....

3. La tarte aux pommes n'a pas l'air bonne. Elle va plutôt prendre la glace à la vanille.

....

4. – Je préfère généralement prendre le métro mais ce soir je préfère prendre le bus.

....

– Et si on partageait un taxi ? ....

5. Est-ce que tu pourrais me donner un coup de main ?

....

Donner un conseil

On peut exprimer le conseil à l'aide de **should**, **ought to** et **had better**.

	Formation	Utilisation
should	Se conjugue de la même façon à toutes les personnes. **FA** : **I /.../ they should** + BV Ex. : **She should take a holiday** **FI** : **Should I /.../ they** + BV? Ex. : **Should we take a holiday?** **FN** : **I /.../ they shouldn't** + BV Ex. : **I shouldn't take a holiday**	S'emploie pour donner un conseil plutôt subjectif. Ex. : **You should really be kinder to your mother**, *Tu devrais vraiment être plus gentil(le) avec ta mère* Pour atténuer le côté directif de **should**, on l'emploie souvent avec **maybe**, qui signifie *peut-être*. Ex. : **Maybe you should smoke less**, *Tu devrais peut-être fumer moins*
ought to	**Ought to** s'utilise quasiment toujours à la **FA** et a la même conjugaison pour les personnes : **I /.../ they ought to** + BV.	S'utilise pour ce qui relève du devoir, de la bienséance ou de la morale. Ex. : **You/he ought to respect teachers**, *Tu devrais / il devrait respecter les professeurs*
had better	**Had better** s'utilise davantage aux **FA** et **FN**. On utilise la même conjugaison à toutes les personnes : **FA** : **I /.../ they had better** + BV Ex. : **We'd better eat less chocolate** **FI** : **Had I /.../ they better** + BV? Ex. : **Had he better eat less chocolate?** **FN** : **I /.../ they had better not** + BV Ex. : **She'd better not eat so much chocolate**	Il signifie *tu ferais mieux de...* Par rapport à **should**, **had better** exprime en plus une mise en garde, qui est parfois mentionnée. Elle est alors formulée dans une proposition introduite par **or** (*ou*) ou **or else** (*ou sinon*). Ex. : **You'd better eat less chocolate or you'll be sick**, *Tu ferais mieux de manger moins de chocolat ou tu vas être malade*

NB :
- **Should** et **had better** sont souvent utilisés à la forme interro-négative. Ex. : **Shouldn't you call the police?** *Ne devrais-tu pas appeler la police ?* **Hadn't we better buy a new car?** *Est-ce qu'on ne ferait pas mieux d'acheter une nouvelle voiture ?*
- **Had better** convient mieux pour un conseil dans une situation particulière alors que **should** convient aussi pour les situations générales. Ex. : **You should always tell your friends the truth but this time you'd better not because it would hurt Anna**, *Tu devrais toujours dire la vérité à tes amis mais cette fois tu ferais mieux de ne pas le faire car cela blesserait Anna.*

30 Corrige les erreurs de construction éventuelles.

1. Shouldn't she take an umbrella? It's going to rain.

....

2. You ought respect the highway code.

....

3. We had better not to spend so much money.

....

4. She should going to the hairdresser's.

....

5. You ought to switching off your phone in hospitals.

....

6. They had better stop smoking.

....

31 Réécris cette phrase en utilisant des formes pleines.

She'd better save some money but she'd rather spend it during the sales.

....

32 Formule des phrases comparant ce que Sophie devrait faire mais qu'elle préfère faire...

Elle devrait...	mais elle préfère...	
1. se reposer	voyager beaucoup	**1.** ....
2. faire sa lessive	promener son chien	**2.** ....

33 Passe les phrases suivantes à la FI puis à la FN.

1. We had better get some sleep. FI .... ?

FN ....

2. They had rather tell him. FI .... ?

FN .... ?

À qui sont destinés les conseils et recommandations suivants ?

⬜ Anna feels dizzy.	⬜ David is very lonely.	⬜ John says "silly cop!"
⬜ Jim is eating with his fingers.	⬜ Liam has got a bad report.	⬜ Kelly doesn't know what to do.

1. "Maybe you should see the careers adviser"

2. "You ought to respect table manners"

3. "You had better see a doctor"

4. "Maybe you should work more"

5. "You ought to respect the police"

6. "Maybe you should socialize more"

35 **Construis des énoncés pertinents avec had better et or à partir des éléments suivants.**

1. study more – fail your exam

....

2. not forget your coat – you be cold

....

36 **Traduis les phrases suivantes.**

1. Tu ferais mieux de ne pas chatter en ligne avec des inconnus.

....

2. Tu devrais payer tes impôts.

....

3. Ton nez coule. Tu devrais peut-être te moucher.

....

La valeur de probabilité des modaux

Les modaux expriment certaines modalités de l'action (le nécessaire, l'obligatoire, par exemple), mais ils servent aussi à évoquer la probabilité. Nous avons déjà partiellement abordé la question avec **must**, creusons un peu…

0 %   **might**   **may**   **should**   **must**   100 % de chances

- **might** : 10 % de chances (*il se pourrait que, on ne sait jamais*). Ex. : **It might rain during the summer in Morocco – but it's really improbable**
- **may** : 50 % de chances (*il se peut que*). Ex. : **I'm going to hurry up but I may be late**
- **should** : 70 % de chances (*selon toute logique, d'après mes calculs*). Ex. : **It takes two hours to get there, she should be there now**
- **must** : 90 %, c'est presque sûr (*ça doit être…*). Ex. : **They've just bought a beautiful house, they must be happy**

37 Classe les élèves du plus au moins susceptible d'avoir son examen et complète les phrases 1 et 3 avec le prénom qui convient.

0 %   …………   Eric   …………   Adam   100 %

1. ……… is generally a good student but he can have bad marks too.

2. Henry always has poor marks. But you never know.

3. ……… is a straight-A student. I'm sure he will pass.

4. Lucy is a good student on average. I can't see any reason why she can fail.

38 Construis des phrases avec **must, should, may** ou **might** selon le degré de probabilité indiqué.

1. It's raining but she ……………………… be hiking (10 %)

2. She passed her exam. She ………………………… be in a good mood (90 %)

3. Some workers are angry. They …………………………… go on strike (50 %)

4. She was so worried. She …………………………… be relieved now (70 %)

Traduis les phrases suivantes.

1. Il se peut qu'elle fonde en larmes quand tu lui apprendras la nouvelle.

....

2. Elle a eu son examen hier, elle doit être tellement soulagée !

....

Banque de mots Quelques prépositions spatiales	**around** [ᵉᵘ'ra-ound], *autour de*	**next to** ['nèkst tᵉᵘ], *à côté de*	Autres mots **beach** ['bitch], *plage*
across [ᵉᵘ'kros], *à travers*	**away from** [ᵉᵘ'ouèï frᵉᵘm], *loin de*	**opposite** ['opᵉᵘzit], *en face de*	**to breathe** ['briDH], *respirer*
against [ᵉᵘ'gènst], *contre*	**behind** [bi'Haïnd], *derrière*	**over** ['ᵉᵘouvᵉᵘr], *par-dessus*	**careful** ['kèᵉᵘfᵉᵘl], *prudent*
along [ᵉᵘ'long], *le long de*	**between** [bi'touin], *entre*	**through** ['THrou], *à travers (un obstacle)*	
	far from ['fâ frᵉᵘm], *loin de*	**towards** [tᵉᵘ'ouôdz], *vers*	

 **Entoure la bonne préposition.**

1. Put your racket against – along – across the door.

2. The temperatures are going to be well above – towards – along zero.

3. You must be careful when walking against – around – across the street.

4. I can't breathe through – over – above my nose.

Remets les lettres dans l'ordre pour retrouver la préposition utilisée dans les phrases suivantes, puis propose une traduction.

1. Could you sit XENT OT .... me?

.... ?

2. I would rather not live RAF YAWA .... from my friends.

....

3. In Japan, wives ought to walk BNEDIH .... their husbands.

....

4. I'd better sit NEBTEWE .... Ian and Jane, they're always arguing!

....

Traduis les phrases suivantes.

1. Il se peut que son appartement soit en face de la gare.

....

2. Peux-tu sauter par-dessus le mur ?

....

3. Les enfants devraient rester éloignés du feu et ne pas courir autour de la piscine.

....

4. Demain, nous serons en train de marcher le long de la plage.

....

Bravo, tu es venu à bout de la deuxième unité ! Il est maintenant temps de comptabiliser les icônes et de reporter le résultat en page 128 pour l'évaluation finale.

Unité 3
Exprimer des situations passées

Le prétérit

Le prétérit permet d'évoquer une action passée et terminée, sans aucun lien avec le présent. Cette action est souvent datée ou accompagnée d'un marqueur de temps passé précis (voir Banque de mots). Il existe une forme simple et une forme **-ing** du prétérit.

Prétérit simple

• Pour les verbes réguliers :

FA : **I /.../ they** + BV + **-ed**

Ex. : **I/she/they watched the game last night**

FI : **Did I /.../ they** + BV?

Ex. : **Did I/she/they watch the game last night?**

FN : **I /.../ they didn't** + BV

Ex. : **I/she/they didn't watch the game last night**

• Pour les verbes irréguliers (p. 121) :

À la **FA**, leur prétérit est une forme fixe à apprendre.

FA : **I/she/they went** (preterit de **to go**) **to Boston last month.**

FI : **Did I/she/they go to Boston last month?**

FN : **I/she/they did not (didn't) go to Boston last month**

• To be :

FA : **I/she/he/it was, we/you/they were.**

FI : **Was I/she/he/it? Were we/you/they?**

FN : **I/she/he/it wasn't, we/you/they weren't**

• Usage particulier du prétérit simple : dans les phrases exprimant le conditionnel.

Ex. : **If I knew, I would tell you,** *Si je (le) savais, je te (le) dirais*

La forme conditionnelle de **to be** est **were** à toutes les personnes.

Ex. : **If I were you, I would not work so much,** *Si j'étais toi, je ne travaillerais pas autant*

Prétérit -ing

• Utilisation : pour parler d'une action en déroulement dans le passé, qui peut être interrompue par une autre action passée au prétérit simple. Dans ce cas, on l'emploie parfois avec **while**, qui signifie *pendant que.*

Ex. : **It rained while I was sleeping,** *Il a plu pendant que je dormais*

• Formation :

FA : sujet + **to be** au prétérit + BV **-ing**

Ex. : **You were reading when I arrived,** *Tu étais en train de lire quand je suis arrivé*

FI : **to be** au prétérit + sujet + BV **-ing**?

Ex. : **Was she reading when I arrived?**

FN : sujet + **to be** au prétérit + **not (wasn't/weren't)** + BV **-ing**

Ex. : **We weren't reading when you arrived**

• To be :

FA : **I/she/he/it was being, we/you/they were being.**

FI : **Was I/she/he/it being? Were we/you/they being?**

FN : **I/she/he/it wasn't being, we/you/they weren't being**

Banque de mots

to begin [bi'gin], *commencer*

bruise ['brouz], *bleu (coup)*

to bump into ['beump int^eu], *tomber sur quelqu'un par hasard*

to catch a cold ['katch ^eu 'k^euould], *attraper un rhume*

choir ['kouaï^eur], *chorale*

to come over ['keum '^euouv^eur], *passer chez quelqu'un*

to cough ['cof], *tousser*

exhibition [èkzi'bich^eun], *exposition*

to fail an exam ['fèïl ^eun 'igzam], *échouer à un examen*

to forget [f^eu'gèt], *oublier*

to get pregnant ['gèt 'prègn^eunt], *tomber enceinte*

gorgeous ['gôdj^eus], *magnifique*

to grow a moustache ['gr^eou ^eu m^eu'stâch], *faire pousser une moustache*

to happen ['Hap^eun] / **to take place** ['tèïk 'plèïs], *se passer*

high school ['Haï skoul], *lycée*

to leave ['liv], *partir, quitter*

to make up ['mèïk ^eup], *se réconcilier*

market ['mâkit], *marché*

to miss a step ['mis ^eu 'stèp], *rater une marche*

to retire [ri'taï^eur], *partir à la retraite*

to scold ['sk^euould], *gronder*

to sleep ['slip], *dormir*

Marqueurs de temps prétérit

ago [^eu'g^eou], *il y a …*

during ['diouring] + événement, *pendant …*

in + année, *en* + année

last week, month, year ['last 'ouik, 'meunTH, 'i^eur], *la semaine, le mois, l'année dernier(ère)*

yesterday ['ièst^eudèï], *hier*

---

1 Vocabulaire — entoure la bonne reformulation. ●●

1. I didn't remember.
a. I forgot
b. I remembered
c. I came over

2. I came over to my friends'.
a. I helped them
b. I visited them
c. I scolded them

3. Ian and I made up.
a. We married
b. We traveled
c. We stopped arguing

4. My teacher retired.
a. He stopped working
b. He forgot something
c. He scolded us

5. I caught a cold.
a. I was sick
b. I had a baby
c. I stopped working

6. He missed a step.
a. He forgot something
b. He was sick
c. He fell down the stairs

---

2 Complète les phrases suivantes avec was, wasn't, were ou weren't. ●●

1. I .... as pretty as my sister when we .... children.

2. .... the police here when the accident happened?

3. The pizza .... very good. I didn't like it.

4. If I .... (be) rich, I would buy a large house.

5. Dan and I .... married from 1999 to 2009.

6. You .... keen on bowling in high school. You hated it.

3 Max raconte à son correspondant ce qu'a fait sa famille la semaine passée, mais il ne maîtrise pas toujours bien les verbes irréguliers. Corrige ses erreurs éventuelles.

1. I played tennis with Mark and he won.

....

2. The neighbour's dog bited my sister. My parents called the doctor.

....

3. We eated the cookies you sent me. They were delicious.

....

4. My brother Erik bought a new guitar. It costed him 500 euros.

....

5. My father went fishing and catched some big fish.

....

6. I forgot to do my homework and my teacher punished me. But I learned my irregular verbs.

....

7. I fought with the neighbour's son. My parents forbided me to see him anymore.

....

8. My sister dreamt that Beyonce was her best friend.

....

9. My brother lent me his mp3 player because I breaked mine.

....

10. My sister drew a nice portrait of me and I readed a detective story.

....

4 Mets les phrases suivantes au prétérit simple.

1. We work in a charity shop.

....

2. She breaks her leg while skiing.

....

3. Does your husband retire in 2016?

....

4. Sarah gives her phone number to strangers.

....

5. Do they sing in a choir at school?

....

5 Construis des phrases au prétérit à l'aide des éléments suivants. ••

1. Mr Anderson teach English he be young

....

2. My parents sell our house last year

....

3. She not meet the President yesterday

....

4. The company cancel our flight an hour ago

....

5. They intend to move out?

....

6. I write a poem for you last week

....

6 Passe les phrases suivantes à la forme indiquée entre parenthèses. ••

1. I saw Anna at the station yesterday.

(FN) ....

2. Did you leave your umbrella at home?

(FA) ....

3. We slept for ten hours last night.

(FI)...

4. They did not drink any alcohol at the party.

(FA) ....

5. You were spending your holidays abroad.

(FI) ....

6. I would travel less if I had children.

(FI) ....

7 Conjugue les verbes indiqués entre parenthèses au prétérit simple ou progressif. ••

1. I .... (cheat) when the teacher .... (scold) me.

2. He .... (not/run) when he .... (sprain) his ankle. He .... (walk).

3. I .... (know) all the irregular verbs two years ago but I .... (forget) a lot last year.

4. I would not put so much pepper in the sauce if I .... (be) you.

5. If she .... (be) nicer, I would help her.

6. They would be very angry if someone .... (steal) their car.

8 Pour chaque phrase, pose la question qui permet d'obtenir la réponse soulignée. ● ●

1. .... ?

We <u>were sleeping</u> when you called.

2. .... ?

<u>I'm not your mother but I would punish you!</u>

3. .... ?

She bought this new computer <u>two months ago</u>.

4. .... ?

My mother was <u>a nurse</u> from 1980 to 2000.

5. .... ?

They were <u>going to the supermarket</u> when the accident happened.

Permission, capacité et obligation au passé

	Formation	Utilisation
be able to	FA : sujet + **was/were** + **able to** + BV Ex. : **I was able to run 10 miles** FI : **Was/were** + sujet + **able to** + BV? Ex. : **Were you able to run 10 miles?** FN : sujet + **wasn't/weren't** + **able to** + BV Ex. : **She wasn't able to run 10 miles**	FA, FI : capacité temporaire FN : incapacité temporaire
could	FA : sujet + **could** + BV Ex. : **I could run 10 miles when I was younger** FI : **Could** + sujet + BV? Ex. : **Could you run 10 miles when you were younger?** FN : sujet + **could not (couldn't)** + BV Ex. : **She coudn't run 10 miles when she was younger**	FA, FI : capacité durable FN : incapacité durable
have to	FA : **had** (prétérit de **have**) **to** + BV à toutes les personnes Ex. : **We had to leave early** FI : **Did** + sujet + **have to** + BV? Ex. : **Did you have to leave early?** FN : sujet + **did not** + **have to** + BV Ex. : **They didn't have to leave early**	FA, FI : obligation FN : absence d'obligation
be allowed to	FA : sujet + **was/were allowed to** + BV FI : **Was/were** + sujet + **allowed to** + BV? FN : sujet + **wasn't/weren't allowed to** + BV Ex. : **We were not allowed to take the dog**	FA, FI : permission FN : absence de permission

9 Apporte les modifications rendues nécessaires par l'ajout des éléments en gras.

1. I have some time, so I can help you. .... **yesterday, so** ....

2. She feels sick and must stay home. .... **a few hours ago** and ....

3. I can not swim well. **When I was a child**, ...

4. Must she come over? Why .... she .... **when I was sick?**

5. Workers may not retire at 60. **In 1960**, workers ....…..................

Used to et would

Ils permettent d'exprimer l'habitude au passé.

Used to établit un contraste entre une situation passée et présente, la situation passée n'étant plus vraie dans le présent.

FA : sujet + **used to** + BV

Ex. : **I/she/they used to smoke**, *Je/elle/ils fumaient* – sous-entendu, *mais plus maintenant*

FI : **Did** + sujet + **use to** + BV +?

Ex. : **Did you use to smoke?**

FN : sujet + **didn't** + **use to** + BV

Ex. : **We didn't use to like oysters**

Si l'on veut/doit expliciter l'idée de *ne plus*, on utilise soit **no longer** + BV à la **FA**,

soit **not ... any more** ou **not** ... **any longer** + BV à la **FN**.

Ex. : **I used to live in a block of flats in the town center but I don't anymore / but I no longer do. I moved out in a house in the suburbs last year,** *Avant j'habitais un immeuble du centre-ville mais plus maintenant. J'ai déménagé dans une maison en banlieue l'année dernière*

Would, dit « itératif », permet d'exprimer une tendance dans le passé.

Ex. : **On Sundays, he would visit his parents,** *Le dimanche, il allait voir ses parents*

10 Relie chaque début de phrase à la suite qui lui correspond.

1. I used to eat junk food when I was a teenager.	●	●	**a.** to church on Sundays.
2. Did you	●	●	**b.** I would grow a moustache.
3. She would	●	●	**c.** see that horror film?
4. Were you	●	●	**d.** But I no longer do. I eat better now.
5. If I were a man	●	●	**e.** having a good time when we arrived?
6. My grandparents would go	●	●	**f.** not cook much during the week. She did not like it much.
7. This time a month ago, I was	●	●	**g.** take a taxi. Our car broke down this morning.
8. I exercised a lot last year and I was	●	●	**h.** I would exercise more.
9. If I had enough time,	●	●	**i.** visiting Australia.
10. We went	●	●	**j.** Now I do.
11. I did not use to eat oysters when I was young.	●	●	**k.** able to run a marathon.
12. We had to	●	●	**l.** to Spain last year.

11 Transforme les énoncés suivants en utilisant une autre façon de dire **ne plus**.

1. I no longer go to painting exhibitions → ....

2. We don't sing in a choir any more → ....

12 Forme des phrases à partir des éléments fournis, comme dans les exemples suivants.

I/go to the cinema on Sundays
→ I used to go to the cinema on Sundays but I no longer do.

1. we/go to work by bus ....

....

2. My mother/drink a lot of coffee ....

....

you/shopping alone? No – I go with Jane
→ Did you use to go shopping alone? No, I didn't use to. I used to go with Jane.

3. They/like painting exhibitions? No - they prefer hiking ....

....

4. The Jones/scold their children? No - they spoil them a lot ....

....

my brother/be single/marry two years ago
→ my brother used to be single but he married two years ago.

5. We/have no car/buy one last year ....

....

Traduis les phrases suivantes.

1. Étais-tu en train de faire de l'exercice quand je suis passé ?

....

2. Nous sommes tombés sur Emma au marché il y a deux jours.

....

3. Avant j'allais au cinéma tous les vendredis (*mais plus maintenant*).

....

4. Nous allions au restaurant ensemble (*c'est une tendance que nous avions*).

....

5. Nous ne sommes pas allés au musée la semaine dernière.

....

6. Si j'étais toi je ne réprimanderais pas les enfants.

....

7. Son mari serait-il beau s'il avait une barbe ?

....

Les pronoms réfléchis

- Formation : **my-, your-, her-, him-, it-self your-, our-, them-selves**

Ils se placent après le verbe.

- On les utilise pour :

→ insister sur le fait que l'on a réalisé quelque chose soi-même

Ex. : **I have called her myself,** *Je l'ai appelée moi-même*

→ exprimer le *s'/se* des verbes pronominaux français

Ex. : **We enjoyed ourselves,** *Nous nous sommes amusés*

- Attention cependant car de nombreux verbes anglais ne sont pas pronominaux alors que leur équivalent français l'est : **to feel, to get up, to hurry up, to shave, to wake up, to wash, to get dressed, to relax, to sit, to realise.**

- Expressions à connaître : **help yourself,** *servez-vous,* **make yourself at home,** *faites comme chez vous.*

Banque de mots

assignment [ᵉᵘ'saïnmᵉᵘnt], *devoir (à faire à la maison)*

blood ['bleud], *sang*

to enjoy [in'djoï] **oneself,** *s'amuser*

to get dressed ['gèt 'drèst], *s'habiller*

to hurry up ['Heuri ᵉᵘp], *se dépêcher*

to introduce [intrᵉᵘ'diou**s**] **oneself,** *se présenter*

to kill ['kil], *tuer*

to realise ['riᵉᵘlaïz], *se rendre compte de*

to relax [ri'laks], *se détendre*

to take care ['tèïk 'kèᵉᵘr] **of oneself,** *prendre soin de soi*

14 Forme un énoncé logique (1 à 3) ou complète les espaces (4 à 6) en utilisant le pronom réfléchi qui correspond.

1. Your mother did not make the pie for you. You ....

2. I did not do my brother's assignment. He ....

3. Our father did not buy us a computer. We ....

4. She did not cook the Indian food .... She ordered from the restaurant.

5. They did not do the cleaning all by ...., it was too much work.

6. I cut .... while I was gardening yesterday. There was blood everywhere!

15 Comment traduirais-tu ces énoncés ?

1. Il se regarda dans le miroir et se trouva vieux.

....
....
....

2. Elle n'est pas gentille. Nous nous en sommes rendu compte ce matin.

....
....
....

3. Nous avons bien pris soin de nous.

....
....
....

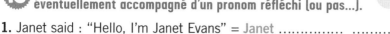

16 Reformule les phrases suivantes à l'aide d'un verbe éventuellement accompagné d'un pronom réfléchi (ou pas...).

1. Janet said : "Hello, I'm Janet Evans" = Janet ....

2. He committed suicide = he ....

3. They put some clothes on = **they** ....

4. We had fun = we ....

5. I had some rest = I ....

6. We did not take our time, on the contrary = **we** ....

Le present perfect (2/2)

- Formation : **have** + participe passé (voir unité 1, p. 19 pour les **FA**, **FI**, **FN**).

Nous avons vu dans l'unité 1 que le **present perfect** pouvait servir à exprimer une action commencée dans le passé et toujours en cours dans le présent (donc traduite par un présent).

- Ce temps s'utilise aussi :

- pour une action passée dont le moment / la date est inconnu(e) ou n'a pas d'importance mais dont les conséquences dans le présent importent.

Ex. : **I have broken my glasses,** *J'ai cassé mes lunettes.* On ne sait pas quand et peu importe, cela signifie davantage **I can't see** ou **I need new ones** par exemple.

- pour faire un bilan sur ses expériences, avec les adverbes **ever**, **already**, **never** ou **yet**.

Ever : s'utilise à la **FI** entre **have** et le p.p. pour demander si on a déjà fait quelque chose au moins une fois dans sa vie.

Ex. : **Have you ever been to China?** *Es-tu déjà allé en Chine ?*

Already : s'utilise entre **have** et le p.p. à la **FA** (dire ce qui a déjà été fait) et à la **FI** (demander ce qui a déjà été fait).

Ex : **Have you already done your homework?** *As-tu déjà fait tes devoirs ?*

Yet : on l'utilise en fin de phrase dans les formes interrogatives et négatives pour demander si quelque chose a déjà été fait, mais dans un délai plus court qu'avec **already**.

Ex. : **Has she had breakfast yet?** *A-t-elle (déjà) pris son déjeuner ?* **She hasn't had breakfast yet**, *Elle n'a pas encore pris son petit déjeuner.*

Never : entre **have** et le p.p., signifie *jamais*.

Ex. : **They've never been married,** *Ils n'ont jamais été mariés.*

- pour évoquer un événement récent, avec l'adverbe **just**, qui se place entre l'auxiliaire et le p.p. Ex. : **I've just called her**, *Je viens de l'appeler.*

Banque de mots

ceiling ['siling], *plafond*

cellar ['sèl^{eur}], *cave*

century ['sèntri], *siècle*

to recover [ri'kov^{eur}], *se remettre d'une maladie, guérir, aller mieux*

remote control ['rim^{eu}out k^{eu}ntr^{eu}oul], *télécommande*

17 Corrige les erreurs éventuelles dans les phrases ci-dessous.

1. I have forgotten to buying stamps.

....

2. Have you ever see a UFO?

....

3. Have they been allowed to open the presents?

....

4. Have they taken yet a shower?

....

5. We have never eat snails.

....

6. He hasn't began his homework yet.

....

18 Passe les phrases suivantes à la forme indiquée entre parenthèses.

1. You have forgotten these old shoes in the cellar.

(FI) ....

2. Has he begun repainting the ceiling?

(FN) ....

19 Complète les phrases suivantes avec **ever**, **already**, **yet**, **never** ou **just**.

1. My brothers have .... read Harry Potter. They don't read.

2. Have you .... played cricket?

3. You needn't call her. I have .... done it.

4. I've .... been to the gym. I'm tired.

5. Have you had dinner .... ?

20 Réponds aux questions suivantes en utilisant **already** ou **never**.

1. Have they ever been afraid of blood before?

Yes, ...

2. Have you ever wanted to live in the 18th century?

No, ...

21 Complète le tableau suivant comme dans l'exemple fourni.

Have they ever been to Canada?	Yes, they went there last winter.
1. you/see the President	Yes/this morning ....
2. She/try Swedish food	Yes/yesterday ....
3. he/buy a scooter	Yes/two days ago ....

22 Associe la bonne action au bon résultat ou l'inverse à partir des propositions suivantes (comme dans l'exemple).

c. is/empty/fridge/the   **e.** has/read/never/he/Harry Potter   **a.** car/serious/he's/accident/a/had

d. anymore/not/he's/single   **b.** if/okay/she's/do/you/know?

Action dans le passé	→ Résultat dans le présent
He has cheated	Him/teacher/punished/the → the teacher punished him
1	He doesn't know what a "muggle" is
2. I haven't done the shopping yet	....
3.	He's disabled now
4. He has got married	....
5. Have you already called Emma?	....

23 Complète les phrases ci-dessous avec **so** ou **because**.

1. Mum has forgotten to buy some tomato sauce .... she cannot make a pizza.

2. He must walk with crutches .... he has sprained his ankle.

3. We haven't saved enough money yet .... we cannot buy a new car.

4. There is blood in the bathroom .... Dad has cut himself.

24 Comment traduirais-tu les phrases suivantes ?

1. Nous n'avons pas encore vu l'exposition.

....

2. J'ai raté une marche, j'ai des bleus.

....

3. Ma sœur vient d'attraper un rhume. Elle a toussé toute la nuit.

....

....

4. As-tu déjà été mariée ?

....

5. Elle n'a jamais réprimandé ses enfants.

....

6. As-tu vu la télécommande ?

....

25 Relie les phrases entre elles comme dans l'exemple.

I/be slimmer – start exercising : I've been slimmer since I started exercising.

1. she/sleep better – decide to take sleeping pills

....

....

2. he/be nicer – get married

....

....

26 Transforme les phrases comme dans l'exemple et propose une traduction de chacun de tes énoncés.

I saw Henry a week ago	=	it has been a week since I saw him *cela fait une semaine que je l'ai vu*	=	I have not seen him for a week *je ne l'ai pas vu depuis une semaine*
1. I smoked a cigar two days ago	=	....	=	....
2. We went to the doctor's last year	=	....	=	....

27 Pose la question qui permet d'obtenir la réponse suivante.

1. .... ? I've seen this film 4 times.

2. .... ? I've slept for 12 hours!

Superlatif (le + ..., le - ...)

On l'emploie très fréquemment au present perfect, accompagné de **ever** à la **FA**.

Ex. : **He is the cutest baby I have ever seen,** *C'est le bébé le plus mignon que j'aie jamais vu*

Superlatif de supériorité

- Adjectif court : **the** + adj. + **-est**

  Ex : **the brightest**
- Adjectif long : **the** + **most** + adj.

  Ex : **the most interesting**

Superlatif d'infériorité

The least + adj. À noter que pour les adjectifs courts, l'anglais préférera souvent employer un superlatif de supériorité avec l'adjectif opposé.

Ex. : **the least thin = the fattest, the least intelligent = the most stupid**

Formes irrégulières : **good : the best, bad : the worst, far : the furthest**

28 **Transforme les phrases suivantes en procédant comme dans l'exemple.**

We have never seen a more handsome man :
he is the most handsome man we have ever seen.

1. She has never eaten a sweeter apple :

....

2. I have never bought a less expensive necklace :

....

3. He has never lived in a messier flat :

....

4. Doctors have never seen a more important discovery than vaccines :

....

5. I have never seen a film worse than that one :

....

Les pronoms réciproques

- Ils servent à exprimer une réciprocité. On les utilise pour traduire les verbes pronominaux français (verbes commençant par *se/s'*). **Each other** est employé quand il y a deux personnes impliquées (*l'un l'autre*) et **one another** quand il y en a plus de deux (*les uns les autres*).

Ex. : **Zack and Sam hate each other / Zack, Kate and Sam hate one another,** *ils se détestent*

- Note que certains verbes anglais ne nécessitent pas l'ajout de pronoms réciproques.

Ex. : **to meet** ['mit], *se rencontrer* ; **to argue** ['âgiou], *se disputer* ; **to fight**, *se battre*

 Complète les phrases suivantes par **each other**, **one another** ou **Ø**.

1. You and I have known .... for 20 years.

2. Pupils help .... a lot in this class.

3. They have argued .... a lot since they got divorced.

4. The four sisters have often invited ....

5. Ian and Isa met .... at university.

Les modaux au passé

Pour exprimer un degré de probabilité au passé, on emploie principalement les modaux **must** et **may** suivis de **have** + p.p. Comme au présent, **must** s'utilise pour une probabilité de 90 % et **may** de 50 %.

Ex. : **He may have been tired,** *Il se peut qu'il ait été fatigué* ; **He must have been tired,** *Il devait sûrement être fatigué.*

À cette forme, **might** et **should** prennent une valeur d'irréel :

- **Should have** + p.p. exprime un regret ou un reproche sur un fait passé.

Ex. : **I should have taken that job,** *J'aurais dû accepter cet emploi.*

- **Might have** + p.p. s'utilise pour un reproche ou une suggestion prudents sur un fait passé.

Ex. : **You might have told me you were not coming!** *Tu aurais pu me dire que tu ne venais pas !*

Dans les phrases suivantes, indique ce que le modal passé exprime (regret, reproche, suggestion, probabilité moyenne, probabilité haute).

1. She must have cried a lot when her dog died.

....

2. You might have tidied your bedroom! Now I have to do it myself!

....

3. I shouldn't have watched that film. It was scary!

....

4. I don't know why he's late. He may have missed his bus.

....

5. You look exhausted. Maybe you might get some sleep.

....

6. You should have been nicer to her.

....

Forme une phrase contenant un modal passé en utilisant les informations fournies dans les colonnes 2 et 3.

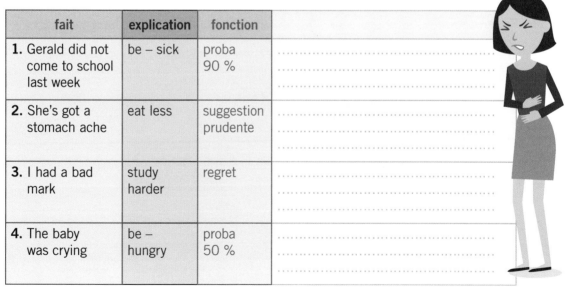

fait	explication	fonction	
1. Gerald did not come to school last week	be – sick	proba 90 %	....
2. She's got a stomach ache	eat less	suggestion prudente	....
3. I had a bad mark	study harder	regret	....
4. The baby was crying	be – hungry	proba 50 %	....

Le cas du present perfect -ing

- Rappel de formation : **have been** + BV **-ing.**
- Utilisation : nous avons vu dans l'unité 1 que le present perfect **-ing** pouvait servir à exprimer une action au présent. Comme pour la forme simple, la forme **-ing** sert aussi à exprimer des actions passées et terminées, dont la date n'a pas d'importance mais qui a des conséquences dans le présent. Il existe cependant deux nuances.

La forme simple met en avant l'accomplissement de la tâche.
Ex. : **I've painted the kitchen,** *J'ai peint la cuisine*

Alors que la forme **-ing** insiste sur l'activité en elle-même et ses aspects perceptibles dans la situation présente.
Ex. : **I've been painting,** *J'ai fait de la peinture* (ça se voit, ça se sent)

Par ailleurs ; la forme **-ing** peut aussi indiquer de l'agacement ou de la colère.
Ex. : **You've been smoking again!** *Tu as encore fumé !* (je le sens…)

Banque de mots
muddy ['meudi], *boueux*
rag ['rag], *chiffon*
slippery ['slip^{eu}ri], *glissant*

 Classe les phrases ci-dessous dans le tableau.

a. I've been cleaning the fridge
b. I've cleaned the fridge

c. I've been running
d. I've run a marathon

1. accent sur l'accomplissement de l'action	2. accent sur l'activité en elle-même
....	....
....	....
....	....
....	....

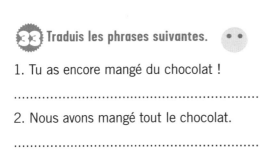 **Traduis les phrases suivantes.**

1. Tu as encore mangé du chocolat !

....

2. Nous avons mangé tout le chocolat.

....

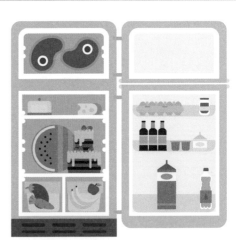

34 Attribue les conséquences dans le présent (a à f) à des faits passés (phrases 1 à 3).

1. I've been dusting the furniture   ....

2. I've been playing rugby   ....

3. I've been cooking some soup   ....

a. you can hear I'm coughing

b. you can see my T-shirt is muddy

c. there are knives and potatoes on the table

d. you can see I'm holding a rag

e. you can see I've got bruises

f. it smells of carrots in the kitchen

35 Imagine deux phrases au present perfect -ing qui pourraient convenir à la conséquence sensible suivante.

Conséquence : The road is slippery.

Causes : ....

....

....

....

Le past perfect

Il sert à relier deux moments du passé. Il existe deux formes :

• Forme simple

- FA : sujet + **had** + p.p.

Ex. : **When you arrived, we had already begun the meeting,** *Quand tu es arrivé, nous avions déjà commencé la réunion*

- FI : **had** + sujet + p.p.**?**

- FN : sujet + **had not (hadn't)** + p.p.

• Forme -ing

Employé avec **for** ou **since**, elle permet de décrire une action en déroulement jusqu'à un moment précis du passé.

- FA : sujet + **had been** + BV -ing

Ex. : **We had been running for an hour when he sprained his ankle,** *Nous étions en train de courir depuis une heure quand il s'est foulé la cheville*

- FI : **had** + sujet + **been** + BV -ing?

- FN : sujet + **had not been** + BV -ing

36 Conjugue les verbes entre parenthèses au past perfect (simple ou continu) ou au prétérit.

1. I ………….. (clean) the fridge for hours when you ……… (to offer) to do it.

2. You …………………. (already have) dinner when I ……………
(to invite) you.

3. …………………………… (you – ever – be) to Spain before you …………..
(go) there last year?

4. She ……………… (feel sick) for months when she …………… (to recover).

37 Complète ce tableau en procédant comme dans l'exemple (propose une traduction des reformulations).

Phrase	→ Reformulation	→ Traduction
He retired before he turned 60.	He had already retired when he turned 60.	Il avait déjà pris sa retraite quand il a eu 60 ans.
1. I met Adam before you introduced us to each other.	………………………………… ………………………………… …………………………………	………………………………… ………………………………… …………………………………
2. ……………………………… ……………………………… ………………………………	I had fallen asleep when the film started.	………………………………… ………………………………… …………………………………

38 Relie les deux parties de manière logique en utilisant le prétérit et le past perfect -**ing**.

1. He – eat for five minutes / break a tooth

………………………………………………………………………………………………

2. We – sing in the same choir for a year / fall in love

………………………………………………………………………………………………

Exprimer le regret avec le past perfect

En plus de **should have** + p.p. mentionné précédemment, on peut exprimer un regret portant sur un fait passé en utilisant le past perfect (simple le plus souvent) dans la structure suivante : sujet + **wish** au présent simple + sujet + **had** + p.p. ou **if only** + sujet + **had** + p.p.

Ex. : **I wish I had taken that job / If only I had taken that job,** *Si seulement j'avais accepté cet emploi*

39 Construis deux phrases exprimant le regret à l'aide des éléments suivants puis propose une traduction.

1. You – come to my party

....

....

Traduction : ....

2. She – not eat this fish

....

....

Traduction : ....

40 Traduis ces phrases.

1. J'avais vu l'exposition quand elle s'est terminée.

....

2. Ils étaient mariés depuis cinq ans quand elle est tombée enceinte.

....

3. Tu avais déjà acheté un billet quand le concert a été annulé.

....

4. Si seulement j'avais été plus sympa avec lui.

....

Bravo, tu es venu à bout de la troisième unité ! Il est maintenant temps de comptabiliser les icônes et de reporter le résultat en page 128 pour l'évaluation finale.

Unité 4
Élargissement et complexification des compétences

Les *question tags*

Les **question tags** sont des petits énoncés interrogatifs de fin de phrase signifiant *non ?, si ?, n'est-ce pas ?, hein ?*

On les forme en inversant le sujet et l'auxiliaire de la phrase de départ (celui qui correspond au temps de cette phrase) et on inverse la polarité : après un énoncé positif, le tag est négatif, et vice versa.

Ex. : **you're Anna's brother, aren't you?** *Tu es le frère d'Anna, non ?*

She didn't dump you, did she? *Elle ne t'a pas largué, si ?*

Ils sont utilisés :

- pour demander confirmation de ce que l'on vient de dire,
- pour marquer la surprise ou l'étonnement,
- pour encourager la conversation et l'échange.

  Ex. : **That coffee isn't good, is it? / You like shrimps, don't you?**

Cas particuliers :

- Lorsque le début d'énoncé contient **never, no, nobody, hardly*, scarcely***, le tag est positif.

  Ex. : **There's no problem, is there?**

- Le question tag pour **I am** est **aren't I**.

  Ex. : **I'm rather handsome, aren't I?**

- Pour atténuer un ordre, on reprend par **will you?**

  Ex. : **Keep quite, will you?**

* signifient *à peine*

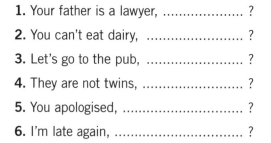

I **Complète ces phrases par le question tag qui convient.** ● ●

1. Your father is a lawyer, ... ?

2. You can't eat dairy, ... ?

3. Let's go to the pub, ... ?

4. They are not twins, ... ?

5. You apologised, ... ?

6. I'm late again, ... ?

7. It has hardly snowed, ... ?

8. You never smoke, ... ?

9. Give me that pen, ... ?

10. He will marry her, ... ?

11. She has got no pets, ... ?

12. That film was not so bad, ... ?

Exprimer la similitude

- Similitude positive (« *Moi /.../ eux aussi* ») : **so** + auxiliaire approprié à la même forme et au même temps que l'énoncé de départ + sujet.

  Ex. : **You like reading. So do I,** *Tu aimes lire. Moi aussi.*

- Similitude négative (« *Moi /.../ eux non plus* ») : **neither** + auxiliaire approprié à la forme opposée et au même temps que l'énoncé de départ + sujet.

  Ex. : **They have not slept yet. Neither has he,** *Ils n'ont pas encore dormi. Lui non plus.*

- **NB** : Dans la vie quotidienne, on emploie souvent **me too** pour *moi aussi* et **me neither** pour *moi non plus.*

2 Reformule la deuxième partie de chaque énoncé, de manière à éviter la répétition.

1. I forgot my keys. They forgot their keys. ....

2. Their son hasn't got a bike. I haven't got a bike ....

3. Sam cannot swim well. Lana cannot swim well. ....

4. Her husband smokes a lot. My sister smokes a lot ....

5. His uncle has bought a laptop. Their daughter has bought a laptop. ....

3 Traduis les phrases suivantes.

1. Ta sœur se plaint toujours, non ? ....

....

2. Ma petite amie est de bonne humeur. Son frère aussi. ....

....

3. Elle n'a pas raté le bus, si ?...

....

Les prépositions

Certains verbes et adjectifs sont suivis d'une préposition. Il n'existe pas de règle pour retenir lesquelles, il faut juste essayer de les retenir lorsque tu apprends les verbes et adjectifs en question.

4 Essaie de deviner par quelle préposition sont suivis les adjectifs suivants.

1. Mark has always been very different of – from – to his brother.

2. My neighbour is angry with – to – of me.

3. Her brother must be interested by – in – about sciences.

4. The school rules are opposed from – of – to smoking.

5. The police said that he was not responsible of – for – with the accident.

5 Les prépositions en rose ont été placées dans la mauvaise phrase. Replace-les dans la phrase qui leur convient.

1. His success **will** depend with the weather. *(Son succès dépendra de la météo.)*

....

2. She has always suffered **for** headaches. *(Elle a toujours souffert de migraines.)*

....

3. Wait **from** me, I'm coming! *(Attends-moi, j'arrive !)*

....

4. This documentary deals **on** poverty. *(Ce documentaire traite de la pauvreté.)*

....

> • Avec les questions commençant par **who, what, which,** la préposition se met en fin de phrase.
> Ex. : **Who are you waiting for?, What is she angry with?**

6 Pose la question portant sur la partie soulignée.

1. My choice will depend on <u>the price</u>.

....

2. I'm interested in <u>geography</u>.

....

3. He suffers from <u>allergies</u>.

....

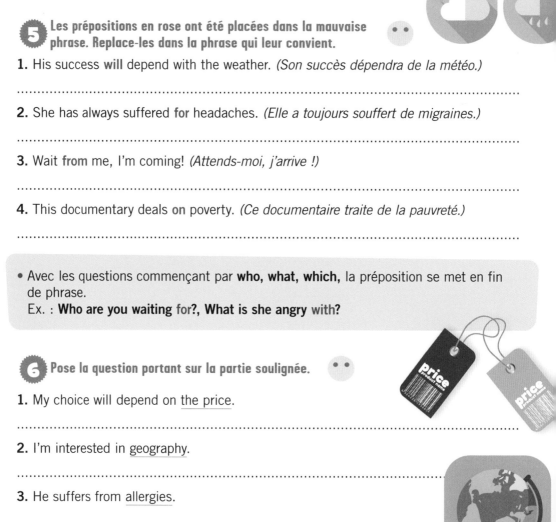

Les *phrasal verbs*

Un **phrasal verb** est un verbe suivi d'une particule (préposition comme **in, on, out** ou adverbe comme **across, away, down,** etc.). La particule donne un sens idiomatique au verbe : l'ensemble verbe + particule signifie autre chose que l'addition du sens du verbe seul et de celui de la particule.

Ex. : **He's showing off with his new shoes.**

Sans **off,** le verbe **to show** signifie *montrer/faire voir* et non *frimer* ! Apprenons-en quelques-uns en faisant les exercices suivants.

7 Déduis le sens de ces **phrasal verbs** à partir de l'exemple d'emploi fourni.

Phrasal verb	Exemple d'emploi	Déduction du sens
1. turn down	They offered him a great job but he turned it down.	....
2. give up	You should give up smoking, it's really bad for you.	....
3. come across	I came across that book at the library.	....
4. run out	We're running out of bread. Can you go to the baker's please?	....
5. break down	I need to go to work on foot because my car has just broken down.	....

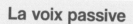

La voix passive

• phrase active :	**The school** Sujet	**will order** verbe (au futur en l'occurrence)	**new computers** COD
• phrase passive :	**New computers** Sujet	**will be ordered** **be** au temps du verbe de la phrase active + p.p. du verbe	**by the school** complément d'agent introduit par **by**

Le complément d'agent n'est pas mentionné quand il n'a pas d'importance ou qu'il n'est pas connu. Dans un certain nombre de cas, on traduit le passif par une tournure impersonnelle.

Ex. : **He was thanked for his help,** *On l'a remercié pour son aide.*

Banque de mots

to build ['bild], *construire*

to buy ['baï], *acheter*

cinnamon ['sinam^{eu}n], *cannelle*

to give ['giv], *donner*

joke ['dj^{eu}ouk], *blague*

to kill ['kil], *tuer*

lie ['laï], *mensonge*

to mug ['meug], *agresser*

to open ['^{eu}oup^{eu}n], *ouvrir*

to sell ['sèl], *vendre*

to send [sènd], *envoyer*

to subtitle ['seubtaït^{eu}l], *sous-titrer*

treatment ['tritm^{eu}nt], *traitement*

8 Complète le tableau suivant.

Phrase active	Phrase passive
1. She...	a pizza is being made
2. I...	a pizza was made
3. They...	a pizza has been made
4. We..	a pizza had been made
5. She...	a pizza would be made

9 Conjugue les verbes donnés entre parenthèses à la voix passive (fais attention aux temps !).

1. Twenty people .... in car accidents every day. **(kill)**

2. The telephone .... by Alexander Bell in 1876. **(invent)**

3. A new school .... next year. **(open)**

4. Spanish .... in many countries. **(speak)**

5. Your cake .... by the children right now. **(eat)**

6. They .... when the war started. **(just be marry)**

7. I .... when the police arrived. **(mug)**

10 Remets les éléments dans l'ordre pour former des phrases passives correctes, puis passe-les à la voix active.

1. a/Moonlight/will/by/be/new/discovered/planet/Professor

....

....

2. not/this/subtitled/teacher/been/film/our/has/by

....

....

Le passif des verbes à deux compléments

Les verbes d'échange **to buy, to give, to offer, to pay, to promise, to sell, to send, to teach, to tell, to write** ont un complément d'objet et un complément de personne (*on offre/donne/dit… quelque chose à quelqu'un*). Il existe deux constructions passives possibles pour ces verbes :

- avec le complément de personne comme sujet (la plus utilisée)

  Ex. : **She gave him/Peter some money → He was given some money**

- avec le complément d'objet comme sujet

  Ex. : **She gave some money to Peter.** Dans ce cas, on met l'accent sur **money → Some money was given to Peter.**

11 Traduis les énoncés suivants.

1. On a découvert un nouveau traitement.

....

2. On nous a donné un beau meuble.

....

12 Transforme les phrases 1-2 pour que l'accent ne soit plus mis sur la personne mais sur l'objet. Fais l'inverse pour les phrases 3-4.

1. I have been sent a strange e-mail.

....

2. You were told a lie.

....

3. A large house will be bought for them.

....

4. A lot of free time is being given to her.

....

13 Complète les phrases suivantes en conjuguant les verbes à l'aide d'un passif.

1. A letter .... to the headmaster right now. (write)

2. You .... a secret soon. (tell)

3. My sister .... a better job last year. (to promise)

4. English .... to my children since 2015. (to teach)

14 Donne les deux formes passives possibles pour ces phrases à la forme active.

1. The farmer gives us eggs every week. ....

....

....

2. The history teacher has given us an assignment. ....

....

....

Le discours indirect

Il s'utilise pour rapporter les paroles de quelqu'un. Le passage du discours direct au discours indirect exige d'adapter le temps (on appelle cela la concordance des temps), les pronoms, ainsi que les indicateurs temporels et spaciaux.

Concordance des temps

Verbe au style direct au...	Se met au style indirect au...
présent* : **I'm quiet**	prétérit* : **he said (that) he was quiet**
prétérit* : **I was quiet**	past perfect* : **he said (that) he had been quiet**
present perfect* : **I have been quiet**	past perfect* : *idem*
futur* : **I will be quiet**	conditionnel* : **he said (that) he would be quiet**
impératif : **Be quiet**	infinitif : **he told me to be quiet**
can : **I can be quiet**	could : **he said (that) he could be quiet**
may : **I may be quiet**	might : **he said (that) he might be quiet**
should : **I should be quiet**	should : **he said (that) he should be quiet**
must : **I must be quiet**	must : **he said (that) he must be quiet**

* La forme (simple ou **-ing**) doit être gardée.

NB : - on utilise plus couramment **to tell** que **to say** pour rapporter des paroles ;
- **that** est optionnel à l'oral ;
- si le verbe introducteur est au présent, les temps ne changent pas, seuls changent les pronoms et indicateurs temporels.
Ex. : **I went to the doctor's yesterday** ➜ **he says (that) he went to the doctor's the day before.**

Changement d'indicateurs temporels et spatiaux

here ➜ there ; yesterday ➜ the day before ; ago ➜ before
last week/month/year ➜ the week/month/year before
next week/month/year ➜ the following week/month/year

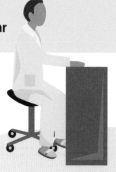

Banque de mots	
to apply for a job [eu'plaï feur eu 'djob], *postuler pour un emploi*	**prejudice** ['prèdjeudis], *préjugé*
to disturb [di'steub], *déranger*	**to warn** ['ouôn], *prévenir*

15 Relie chaque début d'énoncé à sa suite pour former une phrase correcte, puis passe-les au discours direct.

1. Amy says that she ●	●	**a.** could borrow their car.
2. Tom told me that he ●	●	**b.** wife had been ill for 5 years.
3. My mother told me ●	●	**c.** had been shopping there the day before.
4. They told me that he ●	●	**d.** doesn't like cinnamon.
5. Eric said that his ●	●	**e.** to go do my homework.
6. They said that you ●	●	**f.** was going to marry Helena soon.

1. " .... "

2. " .... "

3. " .... "

4. " .... "

5. " .... "

6. " .... "

16 Passe les phrases suivantes au discours indirect.

1. "My ex boyfriend had prejudices."

She says ....

2. "I have been living in France for 10 years."

He said ....

3. "You must not disturb my son."

She said ....

4. "We will go to the opera tomorrow."

He said that ....

5. "Help your mother with the cooking next week."

He told me ....

6. "I'm in love with you."

She said that ....

Les interrogations indirectes

- Elles servent à exprimer *(se) demander si/que/quoi/comment...*
- Il faut faire attention à l'ordre des mots : sujet + **wonder/ask** + mot interrogatif (**if/whether, who, when, where, what, how**) + sujet + verbe.
- On ne met pas de point d'interrogation à la fin d'une interrogation indirecte.

  Ex. : **I wonder what she looks like,** *Je me demande à quoi elle ressemble*

- Lorsque l'interrogation indirecte contient un discours rapporté, la concordance des temps vue plus haut s'applique.

  Ex. : **He asked where you were,** *Il m'a demandé où tu étais*

- **to wonder** ['oueund^eur] **if/whether** ['ouèDH^eur], *se demander si/si oui ou non*

17 Refomule ces énoncés avec une interrogation indirecte.

1. "What's your astrological sign?"

Tell me ....

2. "Does he want to dump her?"

I wonder ....

3. "How tall is your brother?"

I asked him ....

4. "Where are my glasses?"

Do you know .... ?

5. "Don't ask too many questions."

He told me ....

18 Transpose ces interrogations indirectes en interrogations directes.

1. He asked me when they would visit.

" .... "

2. He wondered whether you had been warned or not.

" .... "

3. He'd like to know if he might smoke.

" .... "

4. He told me not to tell my sister.

" .... "

19 Traduis les phrases suivantes.

1. Ton frère m'a dit que tu étais divorcé depuis 2008.

....

2. Nous ne savons pas ce que « swag » signifie.

....

3. Ils m'ont demandé de ne pas te prévenir.

....

Les propositions subordonnées relatives

Elles viennent compléter un nom. Elles sont introduites par un pronom relatif qui représente ce nom. Le choix du pronom dépend de la fonction que remplit le nom dans la proposition principale.

Fonction	Antécédent inanimé	Antécédent animé
Sujet	which, that* Ex. : **the cat which is in the garden is our neighbour's**	who Ex. : **the man who is talking to Mr Hanson is the director**
COD	which, that*, Ø Ex. : **she doesn't like the book Ø I bought her, I hate the film that/which you're watching**	who/that ou Ø Ex. : **the boy (that) she likes is Irish**
	Note que quand le pronom relatif est un complément, il est plus naturel de ne pas le mettre, surtout à l'oral. Ex : **the man Ø she married is handsome**	
Complément de nom (*de... dont*, indique la possession)	whose Ex. : **the book whose cover is black**	whose Ex. : **this is the teacher whose book has been stolen**

* On emploie **that** (ou **Ø**) après un superlatif, **first/last, all** et **only**.
Ex. : **apples are the only fruit that I love**

Autres pronoms relatifs :
- **which** peut reprendre une proposition entière
  Ex. : **He arrived late again, which is impolite**
- **what** : *ce qui, ce que*
  Ex. : **I don't know what she wants**
- **where** : pour reprendre un antécédent désignant un lieu
  Ex. : **This is the factory where I work**
- **when** : pour reprendre un antécédent désignant une date, un moment
  Ex. : **Sunday is the day when most people see their families**
- Quand la phrase contient un verbe à préposition, on la met en fin de proposition.
  Ex. : **This is the man she is in love with.**

Banque de mots

bachelor ['batch^{eu|eur}], *célibataire*

to bury ['bèri], *enterrer*

civil servant ['siv^{eu}l seuv^{eu}nt], *fonctionnaire*

childhood ['tchaïldHoud], *enfance*

cleaning lady ['klining lèïdi], *femme de ménage*

drinking water ['drinking ouôt^{eur}], *eau potable*

factory ['faktri], *usine*

fattening food ['fat^{eu}ning foud], *nourriture qui fait grossir*

to fire ['faï^{eur}], *renvoyer, licencier*

graveyard ['grèïviâd], *cimetière*

in love with ['leuv ouiDH], *amoureux de*

mall ['môl], *centre commercial*

novelist ['nov^{eu}list], *romancier*

opium den ['opi^{eu}m dèn], *fumerie*

to put on weight ['pout on 'ouèït], *prendre du poids*

second-hand ['sèk^{eu}nd Hand], *d'occasion*

skiing/surfing instructor ['skiing/'seufing instreukt^{eur}], *moniteur de ski/surf*

walking stick ['ouôking stik], *canne*

washing powder ['ouôching pa-oud^{eur}], *lessive*

40°

 Complète les phrases suivantes avec les mots de vocabulaire adéquats.

washing powder ; a cleaning lady ; drinking water ; opium dens ; a factory ; a bachelor

1. .... were places where people would smoke opium.

2. .... is a place where some people work.

3. .... is water that you can drink.

4. .... is a man who is not married.

5. .... is a powder whose function is to wash dirty clothes.

6. .... is a lady who does other people's housework.

21 **Complète les phrases suivantes avec un pronom relatif ou Ø (parfois, il y a plusieurs solutions possibles).**

1. You're the only person .... I know .... doesn't like pasta!

2. The graveyard .... my grandparents are buried is in the South of Italy.

3. They fired the cleaning lady, ... was a bad idea. She was a good woman.

4. This is the biggest supermarket .... has opened in the country.

5. I have no idea .... they are talking about.

6. The walking stick .... she is using was made in Germany.

7. Emma, ... mother is a novelist, wants to write as well.

8. Childhood is a time .... people are still innocent.

22 Pour chaque phrase, relie les deux propositions indépendantes par un pronom relatif, puis propose une traduction.

1. I have not put on weight. This is a good thing.

....

....

2. The epidemy happened in the 15th century. People had no drinking water then.

....

....

3. The accident happened in a factory. My father used to work in that factory.

....

....

4. I take classes with a skiing instructor. His eyes are the most beautiful ever.

....

....

5. You bought some washing powder. It smells good.

....

....

6. You think something about me. I don't care.

....

....

Banque de mots

accountant [ᵉᵘ'ka-ountᵉᵘnt], *comptable*

advertising ['advᵉᵘtaïzing], *publicité*

to agree to [ᵉᵘ'gri tᵉᵘ], *consentir à*

architect ['âkitèkt], *architecte*

to be rid ['rid] **of,** *être débarrassé de*

bricklayer ['briklèïᵉᵘr], *maçon*

chemist ['kèmist], *pharmacien*

driving test ['draïving tèst], *permis de conduire*

to go for a run ['gᵉᵘou fᵉᵘr ᵉᵘ reun], *aller courir*

lovely ['leuvli], *charmant*

neighbourhood ['nèïbᵉᵘHoud], *voisinage, quartier*

to pick ['pik] **someone up,** *aller chercher quelqu'un*

to pick up the phone ['fᵉᵘoun], *décrocher le téléphone*

silly ['sili], *bête*

snow ['snᵉᵘou], *neige*

to stop by ['stop baï], *s'arrêter voir quelqu'un*

sunrise ['seunraïz], *lever du soleil*

surgeon ['seudjᵉᵘn], *chirurgien*

Les subordonnées circonstancielles

Elles précisent les circonstances de réalisation d'une action (ses causes, conséquences, buts, etc.).

- Exprimer la cause : on utilise **because** (*parce que*) ou **as/since** (*puisque, vu que*).

  Ex. : **Since she wants to lose weight, she should start a diet.**

- Exprimer la condition : on utilise **if** (*si*), **unless** (*à moins que*), **as long as** (*tant que, du moment que*).

  Ex. : **You could get an A if you worked more. / You won't get an A unless you work more. / You will get an A as long as you work hard.**

- Exprimer le but et la conséquence : on utilise **in order to, to, so as to, so that** (*de façon à*).

  Ex. : **She wakes up early in order to go for a run / so that she could go for a run.**

- Exprimer l'opposition : on utilise **whereas** (*tandis que*), **but** (*mais*), **yet** (*et pourtant*).

  Ex. : **Ian is Welsh whereas Duncan is Irish. / I don't like beer but I like cider. / He's very nice. Yet there's something I don't like about him.**

- Exprimer la concession : **though/although** + proposition verbale (*bien que*), **however** (*cependant*), **in spite of/despite** + nom (*malgré*), **even if/even though** (*même si*).

  Ex. : **Although she is very rich, she lives in a small flat.**

  Dogs are generally not allowed. However, we'll make an exception.

  I want to go out in spite of the rain / despite the rain.

  Even though / Even if she's old, my grandmother exercises a lot.

---

23 **Dans chaque phrase, entoure la conjonction qui permet de former une phrase pertinente.**

1. You can become a surgeon, a chemist or an architect *as long as – unless* you study hard.

2. Keith works in marketing *despite – whereas* his wife works in advertising.

3. We have got up early *in order to – although* see the sunrise.

4. She has decided to go for a run *in spite of – although* the snow.

5. I have always wanted to be a bricklayer. My brother, *however – whereas*, would like to be an accountant.

6. His little brother is silly *despite – but* he's so lovely!

24 Relie ces phrases à l'aide d'une des conjonctions suivantes, puis propose une traduction.

although – as – yet – unless – if

1. You won't be allowed to leave work earlier .... your manager agrees to it.

....

2. He eats like a horse. .... he is very thin!

....

3. .... I was in the neighbourhood I have decided to stop by.

....

4. .... you tell me what your problem is, I may be able to help you.

....

5. .... she drove very well, she failed her driving test.

....

25 Pour chaque énoncé, relie les phrases en choisissant une des conjonctions suivantes (un petit réaménagement est nécessaire pour la phrase 2).

so as to – but – even though

1. We tried to call her. She did not pick up.

....

2. I've done all my homework on Friday. I wanted to be rid of it for the weekend.

....

3. I don't regret helping her. She didn't even thank me.

....

• Attention : on confond souvent **whereas** avec **unlike** + nom ou pronom personnel complément (*contrairement à...*).

Ex. : **Unlike you, I love pop music**

26 Reformule en utilisant **unlike** en 1 et **whereas** en 2.

1. Mia is fluent in English, whereas her sister isn't.

....

2. I run twice a week, unlike my brother.

....

27 Traduis les phrases suivantes.

1. Je me suis levé au lever du soleil pour aller courir.

....

2. Il est passé nous voir en dépit de la neige.

....

3. Si l'architecte et le comptable n'y consentent pas, la campagne publicitaire n'aura pas lieu.

....

4. Vu que ton mur est abîmé, tu vas avoir besoin d'un maçon, pas d'un pharmacien !

....

5. Contrairement à toi, j'ai échoué à mon permis de conduire.

....

Savoir quand utiliser *-ing*, l'infinitif ou la base verbale seule

Base verbale simple

- Après les verbes **to let, to help** ; ex. : **Let me help you,** *Laissez-moi vous aider* ; **He helped the old lady cross the street,** *Il a aidé la vieille dame à traverser la rue.*

- Dans la structure **to make somebody do something** (*faire faire quelque chose à quelqu'un*). Ex. : **My parents made me wash the car,** *Mes parents m'ont fait laver la voiture.*

Infinitif (*to*)

- Avec des verbes exprimant un projet ou un but comme **to wish, to want, would like, to expect, to order, to tell, to help.** Ex. : **I want to watch this film / He told me to call you.**

- Dans les subordonnées infinitives, qui servent à dire que quelqu'un veut que quelqu'un d'autre fasse quelque chose : proposition principale + nom/pronom personnel complément + **to** + BV. Ex. : **I want them to help me,** *Je veux qu'ils m'aident.*

Base verbale –*ing*

- Après les verbes de goût (vu dans l'unité 1) ;

- les prépositions **after, before, without,** l'adverbe **instead of.** Ex. : **Appetite comes with eating,** *L'appétit vient en mangeant* ; **Eat your dinner instead of laughing!**

- les **phrasal verbs** : **keep on, go on.** Ex. : **Keep on trying!** *Continue d'essayer !*

- les verbes de commencement et de fin : **to stop, to start**

- **to avoid.** Ex. : **Avoid swimming after eating**

- **to need**, dans le sens passif de *avoir besoin d'être* + p.p. Ex. : **The car needs washing,** *La voiture a besoin d'être lavée*

- **let's go.** Ex. : **Let's go camping!**

- **to be busy.** Ex. : **I'm busy cooking,** *Je suis occupée à faire la cuisine*

- les expressions **don't mind, can't stand.** Ex. : **I can't stand waiting, she doesn't mind helping**

- **it's no use.** Ex. : **It's no use crying!** *Ça ne sert à rien de pleurer !*

- **NB** : après les verbes de perception, on peut utiliser BV + **ing** ou BV (ex. : **I saw her cry/crying,** *Je l'ai vue pleurer*).

Le cas du verbe *to remember*

• **to remember + -ing** renvoie à un fait passé
Ex. : **I remember taking my wallet,** *Je me souviens d'avoir pris mon portefeuille*

• alors que **to remember to** + BV renvoie à un fait futur. Ex. : **Remember to take your wallet,** *N'oublie pas de prendre ton portefeuille*

Banque de mots

application letter
[apli'kèïch^{eu}n lèt^{eur}],
lettre de candidature

to complain [k^{eu}m'plaïn],
se plaindre

to expect [ik'spèkt],
s'attendre à

(to stay) focused ['f^{eu}ouk^{eu}st]
on, *(rester) concentré sur*

to gossip ['gosip],
faire des commérages

to repair [ri'pè^{eur}], *réparer*

to whine ['ouaïn], *pleurnicher*

to wrap up ['rap ^{eu}p], *emballer*

28 Relie chaque énoncé à la structure qui lui correspond.

1. Did he let you ....•
2. I told him. I remember ...•
3. You expect me ....•
4. Can you help her ....•
5. Please, avoid ....•
6. She wants ....•
7. I've been busy ....•
8. They made us ....•
9. Let's go ....•
10. Don't keep on ....•

• tell him (?)

• **telling him (?)**

• **to tell him (?)**

29 Corrige les erreurs de construction.

1. When your hair needs cut, you have it cut!

....
....

2. His father helpt him to write his application letter.

....
....

3. I would like you to understand this lesson.

....
....

4. We did not expect you arrive so early.

....
....

5. Instead of to whine you should help me repairing the door.

....
....

6. I did not hear her to gossip about you. I was busy cooking in the kitchen.

....
....

30 Remets les mots dans le bon ordre, puis introduis le verbe fourni entre parenthèses au bon endroit, en le conjuguant à la forme qui convient. (BV, BV + **ing**, **to**)

1. class/focused/wants/in/teacher/more/the/us **(be)**

....

2. you/presents/the/could/me/Christmas/help/? **(wrap up)**

....

3. made/lady/the/cleaning/I **(hoover)**

....

4. any/must/application/you/without/write/mistakes/letter/this **(make)**

....

5. Sarah's/would/less/parents/her/like **(whine)**

....

6. Proverbe qui signifie « ce qui est fait est fait » : over/use/no/milk/spilt/it's **(cry)**

....

31 Traduis les phrases suivantes.

français	anglais
1. Ça ne me dérange pas d'emballer les cadeaux. N'oublie pas d'acheter du pain !	....
2.	Stop complaining and stay focused!
3.	I did not expect her to gossip like that!
4. Prendre un verre de lait avant d'aller au lit vous aidera à vous relaxer.	....
5. Tes cheveux avaient besoin d'être lavés !	....
6. Peux-tu m'aider à réparer mon ordinateur ?	....
7.	We were busy writing an application letter.
8.	It's no use whining, you're not eating sweets before having dinner!

Les subordonnées de condition

La subordonnée de condition est introduite par **if**. Son temps va dépendre du temps employé dans la proposition principale. Voilà un récapitulatif :

Temps de la proposition principale	Temps de la proposition subordonnée*
will + BV. **I will play rugby…**	… **if it doesn't rain** (présent)
would + BV. **I would play rugby…**	… **if it didn't rain** (prétérit) ou … **if it had not rained** (past perfect)
would have + BV. **I would have played rugby…**	… **if it had not rained** (past perfect)

* Note que la subordonnée peut très bien être placée en tête de phrase.

32 Conjugue les verbes au temps qui convient.

1. You …………………………… (pass your driving test) if you focused more.

2. I would have tried my new recipe if …………………………… (**you – be hungry**).

3. The road would not be slippery if …………………………… (it – not snow).

4. We …………………………… (borrow their car) if they agree.

33 Kathy fait des reproches à sa copine Emily. Celle-ci justifie son comportement. Essaie de faire des phrases comportant une subordonnée principale et une subordonnée de condition et qui pourraient constituer la réponse complète d'Emily.

Reproche de Kathy	Excuse d'Emily	Phrase complète d'Emily
1. "You didn't come to my party."	"You didn't invite me!"	I would……………………………………… ………………………………………………
2. "You don't stop complaining."	"Be nicer to me in the future!"	I would……………………………………… ………………………………………………
3. "You never help me."	"You never ask me!"	I would……………………………………… ………………………………………………

Ces deux élèves ont toujours une excuse ; traduis ces excuses en anglais, ainsi que la réponse de leur professeur.

1. « J'arriverai à l'heure si les cours ne commençent pas avant 10 heures ! »

....

2. « J'aurais eu une meilleure note si vous aviez expliqué mieux ! »

....

3. « Je ferais un autre métier si je n'aimais pas autant votre sens de l'humour ! »

....

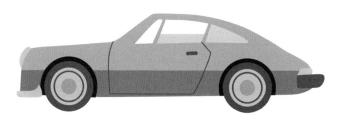

> **Banque de mots**
> **to borrow** ['bor^{eu}ou], *emprunter*
> **to lend** ['lènd], *prêter*
> **slippery** ['slip^{eu}ri], *glissant*

La subordonnée de temps avec sens futur

- Elle est introduite par **when** ['ouèn], **as soon as** [az 'soun az] (*dès que*), **before** [bi'fô^r] (*avant que*), **until** [^{eu}n'til] (*jusqu'à ce que*), **while** ['ouaïl] (*pendant que*).
- **We will go on holidays** ... (futur) → ... **when we have more time** (présent), *Nous irons en vacances quand nous aurons plus de temps*
- **We will not go on holidays** ... (futur) → ... **before we have saved enough money** (present perfect), *Nous n'irons pas en vacances avant d'avoir assez économisé*
- **We stayed up** ... (prétérit) / **We had stayed up** ... (past perfect) → ... **until it got dark** (prétérit), *Nous sommes/étions restés éveillés jusqu'à ce qu'il fasse nuit*

35 Coche la bonne forme grammaticale.

1. You .... video games until you have finished your homework.

a. do not play   **b.** did not play   **c.** will not play

2. We will help you when you .... whining.

a. stop   **b.** stopped   **c.** will stop

3. The accountant asked for you while you .... out.

a. will be   **b.** had been   **c.** were

36 Complète ces phrases par le temps qui convient.

1. She burst out crying when she .... (hear) that he was dead.

2. We.................. (play) rugby again as soon as I feel better.

3. She.................. (not want) to have a baby until they had got married.

4. The cleaning lady.................. (not yet clean) the bathroom when we arrived.

37 Pose la question qui porte sur la partie soulignée.

1. Paul will lend his phone <u>when Damien asks politely</u>.

....

2. My parents <u>will stay in England</u> until they have retired.

....

3. Jim had already been divorced <u>for two years</u> when I met him.

....

38 Traduis les phrases suivantes.

1. Je t'aiderai à écrire ta lettre de candidature quand tu seras plus concentré.

....

2. .... dès que j'aurai emballé les cadeaux.

....

Bravo, tu es venu à bout de la quatrième unité ! Il est maintenant temps de comptabiliser les icônes et de reporter le résultat en page 128 pour l'évaluation finale.

ze

Prononciation

Prononciation

La lettre *a* dans la finale *-age*

Le **a** se prononce [èï] dans les mots d'une syllabe (ex. : **page** [pèïdj]) et le plus souvent [i] s'il fait plus d'une syllabe (ex. : **village** ['vilidj]). Il existe un 3e groupe de mots, pour lesquels elle se prononce [â].

1 Classe les mots fournis dans le tableau selon la prononciation du a dans la finale **-age** et essaie de trouver la règle qui gouverne les mots de ce 3e groupe.

camouflage, cottage, cage, message, collage, manage, image, mirage, damage, sausage, advantage, rage, sabotage, vintage

[èï]	[i]	[â]
....	....	....
....	....	....
....	....	....
....	....	....
....	....	....

La règle est : ....

La lettre *a* dans la finale *-ate*

Elle se prononce :

• [eu] dans les adjectifs et les noms

Ex. : **moderate** ['modeureut], **chocolate** ['tchokleut]

• [èï] dans les verbes

Ex. : **to donate** [deuou'nèït]

2 Place les mots suivants dans le tableau selon la prononciation de leur finale -ate.

climate, desperate, to educate, moderate, to communicate, delicate, senate, private, pirate, to hesitate

[ᵉᵘt]	[èït]
....	....
....	....
....	....

La prononciation du *ch*

Le **ch** peut se prononcer de trois manières différentes :

- la plupart du temps [tch], pour les mots d'origine anglaise ; ex. : **church, choice**

- parfois [k], pour ceux d'origine grecque ; ex. : **Christmas, technician**

- parfois [ch], pour les mots d'origine française ; ex. : **chic**

3 Essaie de classer les mots suivants selon la prononciation de leur ch.

character, chimney, chalet, orchestra, challenge, architect, chaos, cherry, psychology, chauffeur, chair, stomach, monarchy, champagne, cheese, chemistry, mechanic

[tch]	[k]	[ch]
....	....	....
....	....	....
....	....	....
....	....	....
....	....	....

La règle du *magic e*

- V + C finale ou V + 2C ➜ son court : [o], [u], [a], [i], [eu].
  Ex. : **top, put, pack, sit, rock,**

- V + C + e muet ➜ son long : [ᵉᵘou], [iou], [èï], [aï].
  Ex. : **note, mule, cake, mine**

Place la bonne prononciation à côté des mots suivants.

['mad] ['ouaïn] ['kop] ['Heug] ['païn] ['sam] ['sèïm] ['eus] ['i**ou**z] ['ouin] ['Hat] ['Hèït]
['mèïd] ['keut] ['ki**ou**t] ['bit] ['baït] ['k^{eu}oup] ['ouaïn] ['Hi**ou**dj] ['pin] ['ouin]

1. hug ....
2. huge ....
3. cop ....
4. cope ....
5. pin ....
6. pine ....
7. Sam ....

8. same ....
9. bit ....
10. bite ....
11. us ....
12. use ....
13. win ....
14. wine ....

15. cut ....
16. cute ....
17. mad ....
18. made ....
19. hat ....
20. hate ....

**Il existe cependant des exceptions (la plupart sont des mots courants que tu connais).
Entoure-les dans la liste suivante :**

dun – fine – above – love – fin – have – tome – come – mole – some – to live –
time – glove – David – oven – dune – zip – name – Cambridge – divide –
kind – Tom – mind – summit – blind – bone.

Certains sons voyelles sont l'objet de confusions fréquentes.
Abordons quelques exemples dans l'exercice qui suit.

5 En sollicitant le vocabulaire que tu connais et celui croisé dans cet ouvrage, et en
t'appuyant sur les indices donnés en illustration, dis si ces affirmations sont exactes.

a. Le groupe **gh** se prononce toujours [f] (ex. : lau**gh** – enou**gh**.) → *Bien que :* _ _**though**
....

b. Le groupe **oo** se prononce toujours [**ou**] ....

c. Le **ey** se prononce toujours [i] ....

d. Le **ea** se prononce toujours [i] ou [è] ....

e. Le **e** en fin de mot est-il toujours muet ? ....

Le **ea** peut se prononcer de plusieurs manières : [èï], [i], [è], [é^{eu}], [i^{eu}]. Il n'existe pas vraiment de règle, la prononciation de ces mots se retient en les entendant et en les utilisant régulièrement. Tu en connais déjà beaucoup…

6 Les mots courants suivants riment-ils ?

1. great et cheat ☐ Yes ☐ No   **5.** bean et ocean ☐ Yes ☐ No

2. head et bread ☐ Yes ☐ No   **6.** bear et beer ☐ Yes ☐ No

3. great et meat ☐ Yes ☐ No   **7.** fear et pear ☐ Yes ☐ No

4. head et heart ☐ Yes ☐ No   **8.** wear et hair ☐ Yes ☐ No

Prononciation du *h*

Comme tu le sais déjà, le **h** se prononce en début de mot, on le marque par une légère aspiration. Mais il existe des exceptions. Voilà un récapitulatif :

- **Ne se prononce pas**

  - dans quelques mots à connaître ; ex. : **hour**, et d'autres à découvrir dans l'exercice qui suit
  - dans la plupart des mots interrogatifs en **wh**- ; ex. : **what, when, why, which**
  - quand il se trouve à l'intérieur d'un mot ; ex. : **school**. Il y a une exception que tu découvriras dans l'exercice qui suit

- dans quelques mots commençant par **th**- ; ex. : **Thai**
- dans le groupe **gh** de début de mot ; ex. : **ghastly.**

- **Se prononce**

  - la plupart du temps en début de mot ; ex. : **hat, hot, Harry**
  - dans les interrogatifs **who** et **whose**
  - à l'intérieur d'un nom composé, quand le 2e nom commence par un h ; ex. : **doghouse.**

7 Trouve 13 mots contenant un h en t'aidant des indices fournis (et d'un dictionnaire), puis devine dans quels mots le h ne se prononce pas.

1. ☐☐☐☐☐☐☐☐☐☐

2. ☐☐☐☐☐

3. ☐☐☐☐☐☐☐

4. ☐☐☐☐☐

5. utilisé pour interroger sur la cause ☐☐☐

6. utilisé pour interroger sur le lieu ☐☐☐☐☐

7. pas léger… ☐☐☐☐☐

8. fleuve qui coule à Londres ☐☐☐☐☐☐

9. période pendant laquelle il n'y a pas cours ☐☐☐☐☐☐☐☐

10. derrière ☐☐☐☐☐☐

11. héritier ☐☐☐☐

12. honnête ☐☐☐☐☐☐

13. aide ☐☐☐☐

Le *-ed* du prétérit

Il se prononce :

- [t] après les sons /f/, /k/, /p/, /s/, /ch/, /tch/ (le **e** du **-ed** ne se prononce pas) ;
- [d] après autres consonnes (les sons /b/, /DH/, /g/, /v/, /z/, /dj/, /m/, /n/, /l/, /r/, /w/) et toutes les voyelles (le **e** du **-ed** ne se prononce pas) ;
- entre [ᵉᵘd] et [id] après les sons /t/ et /d/.

8 Classe les verbes suivants dans le tableau selon la prononciation de la désinence **-ed**.

missed, retired, bumped, worked, played, ended, looked, killed, applied, whispered, washed, rated, hoped, mixed, complained, whined, snowed, picked, gossiped, expected, repaired

[t]	[d]	[id]/[ᵉᵘd]
....	....	....
....	....	....
....	....	....

L'accent de mot

En anglais, on entend certaines syllabes plus que d'autres. Ces syllabes plus marquées portent l'accent tonique. L'accent est mis sur les mots porteurs de sens (verbes, adverbes, noms, adjectifs) et non sur les mots qui ont juste une fonction d'outil grammatical (prépositions, pronoms, auxiliaires, déterminants*). Dans les représentations phonétiques, la syllabe accentuée est précédée d'une apostrophe (ex : **my 'brother is 'reading in the 'kitchen**). Il existe quelques règles pour t'aider à t'y retrouver :

- les adjectifs et noms de 2 ou 3 syllabes sont accentués sur la première syllabe (ex. : **'carpet, 'funny**), sauf si la dernière syllabe du mot contient **aa, ee, ese, ette, eer, oo, ade** (l'accent porte alors sur cette syllabe). Ex. : **ba'boon, trai'nee, ba'zaar**

- les verbes prennent l'accent sur la 2ᵉ syllabe s'ils en ont plusieurs (ex. : **to de'fine**), à part ceux qui se terminent par **-ow, -en, -y, -er, -ish** (ces derniers sont accentués sur la 1ʳᵉ syllabe). Ex. : **to 'offer**

- pour les noms composés nom + nom, l'accent se met sur le premier nom. Ex. : **'password**

* Cas particuliers : les mots qui ne sont normalement pas accentués peuvent l'être s'ils servent à marquer un contraste.

Ex. : **You don't 'like her. I 'do.**

The 'key is not 'on the 'box, it's 'in the 'box.

It's 'my decision, not yours!

Il existe quelques exceptions que nous allons aborder de plus près dans les exercices (mais que tu trouveras peut-être car certains sont des mots courants que tu as déjà beaucoup entendus).

9 Entoure les noms/adjectifs (a.) et les verbes (b.) mal accentués. ••

a. 'airport, 'bacon, 'candle, book'case, cha'racter, 'breakfast, 'cabbage, 'ice cream, ambu'lance, tooth'paste, 'holiday, presi'dent, 'magical, inno'cent, 'maroon, 'company, en'gineer, fa'mous, 'poverty, bru'nette, Chi'nese, 'funny

b. to de'serve, to em'barrass, to re'move, to re'member, to pu'nish, to 'fasten, to va'ry, to in'crease, to 'follow, to 'banish, to com'plain

10 Les mots courants suivants sont des exceptions à la règle d'accentuation des noms car ils ne sont pas accentués sur la première syllabe. Essaie de deviner où se trouve leur accent. ••

Hello	potato	July
banana	umbrella	eleven
tomato	November	September

L'accentuation des mots suffixés

• les suffixes **-able, -ible, -ism, -ment, -ous, -ly, -er, -ed, -ing** n'ont pas de conséquence sur l'accentuation d'un mot.

Ex. : **'eat – 'eatable, 'pay – 'payment, con'tempt – con'temptible, 'cannibal – 'cannibalism**, etc.

• les suffixes **-ion, -ic(s)** et **-ity** provoquent un déplacement de l'accent de mot sur la syllabe qui les précède.

Ex : **'educate – edu'cation, 'energy – ener'getic, electric – elec'tricity**

11 Classe ces mots dans le tableau et apporte les éventuels correctifs nécessaires. ••

'adaptable, a'greeable, a'voidable, **comprehen'sible**, co'rruptible, re'versible, **cu'bism**, exo'ticism, 'glamourous, **spa'cious**, 'generous, a'mazingly, **pain'ter**, 'accepted, 'working, **im'munity**, cav'ity, eco'nomics, **'politics**, 'ambition, colla'boration, **de'duction**

bien accentué	mal accentué	correction éventuelle
....	....	....
....	....	....
....	....	....

---

 12 Essaie d'accentuer les phrases suivantes.

1. Curiosity killed the cat!

....

2. My neighbour is friendly but he needs to improve his manners.

....

3. My sister's raincoat is gorgeous, isn't it?

....

4. Is your tablet under the sofa or on the sofa?

....

5. My mother-in-law has never sweetened her coffee.

....

6. I was born in September and I'm a wonderful engineer!

....

7. The water on planes is not drinkable.

....

8. The German baby-sitter can't speak English.

....

9. My grandmother's got a lot of affection for her Burmese cat.

....

Le schwa (son [ᵉᵘ])

- C'est le son le plus fréquent en anglais. Les voyelles de syllabes non accentuées se réalisent par ce son. Ex : **listen** ['lisᵉᵘn], **banana** [bᵉᵘ'nanᵉᵘ]).
- Note que les terminaisons -**er**, -**or**, -**ar**, -**re**, -**a**, -**our**, -**ion** et -**ous** se réalisent par ce son.

 **13** Entoure le **schwa** dans les mots suivants.

enormous	amazing	teacher
sugar	agenda	oven
to correct	water	expert
alone	family	postman
education	pasta	about
important	to forgive	doctor
glorious	lemon	to adjust
neighbour	Italian	American

L'intonation de la phrase

- Elle est descendante pour :
  - les phrases à l'impératif,
  - les questions commençant par un interrogatif en **wh-** (**why, where**, etc.),
  - évoquer des informations neutres.
- Elle est montante pour :
  - les questions commençant par un auxiliaire,
  - les questions fermées (auxquelles on répond par *oui* ou *non*),
  - un énoncé partiel, où l'on attend une suite (comme une énumération).

NB : cas des **question tags** :
- descendante si le locuteur pense que l'interlocuteur est d'accord avec lui,
- montante si le locuteur n'en est pas sûr et qu'il demande une véritable confirmation.

14 **Avec quelle intonation prononceras-tu les phrases suivantes ?**

1. We're not late, are we? (*I don't know what time it is*)...

2. There are thirty days in June. ....

3. When are you moving out? ....

4. Don't turn off the light! ....

5. I agree with you. It's too expensive, isn't it? ....

6. Does your brother live in France? ....

7. I'm free on Monday, … ....

8. Were you born in Paris? ....

Les lettres muettes

Certaines lettres anglaises ne se prononcent pas, tu l'as certainement déjà remarqué avec des mots courants comme **listen** ['lis^{eu}n], **talk** ['tôk] ou **know** ['n^{eu}ou]. Voici quelques règles :

lettre	ne se prononce pas…	exemples
b	dans le groupe de lettres **mb** en fin de mot ou si elle précède un **t**	crumb, debt
c	dans le groupe de lettres **sce/sci** ou **scle** en fin de mot	science, crepuscule
d	dans quelques mots à connaître	Wednesday
g	dans le groupe de lettres **gn**	sign
h	dans quelques mots exceptions	hour
k	devant un **n**	knee
l	dans la finale **-ould** et devant **f, k, m**	could, walk, calf, calm
n	dans le groupe de lettres **mn** en fin de mot	autumn
s	devant un **l** dans certains mots	island
t	dans les groupes de lettres **st/stl**	castle
w	devant le **r** et dans quelques mots à connaître	wrong, who

15 Chacun des mots suivants contient une lettre muette ; entoure-la.

comb, muscle, half, solemn, handkerchief, aisle, heir, knife, wrist, gnat, whose, should, doubt, lamb, thumb, whistle, honour

Note sur la phonétique

Dans ce cahier, nous avons utilisé un code phonétique francisé et non le code international, que tu connais peut-être un peu. Cet exercice sera alors une révision. Si tu ne le connais pas, voilà l'occasion de faire connaissance et de t'exercer un peu !

Voici le code phonétique international de l'anglais (les autres consonnes comme **v, t, d,** etc. sont identiques au français) :

Voyelles brèves	Voyelles longues
[æ] **cat**	[ɜ:] **shirt**
[ɪ] **fish**	[u:] **blue**
[e] **bed**	[i:] **key**
[ʊ] **book**	[ɑ:] **car**
[ʋ] **pot**	[ɔ:] **door**
[ə] **a/an**	
[ʌ] **bus**	

Diphtongues	Consonnes
[aɪ] **like**	[h] **hat**
[eɪ] **cake**	[r] **red**
[eə] **chair**	[ð] **the**
[ɪə] **beer**	[ʃ] **English**
[ʊə] **poor**	[j] **yes**
[aʊ] **house**	[w] **what**
[əʊ] **coat**	[ŋ] **long**
[ɔɪ] **boy**	[ʒ] **television**
	[θ] **thank**

16 Quels messages se cachent derrière ces transcriptions phonétiques ?

1. /'ʃʊgə/ ....
2. /'kwaɪət/ ....
3. /ə'meɪzɪŋ/ ....
4. /mɪs'teɪk/ ....
5. /ə'pɒlədʒaɪz/ ....
6. /ʌm'brelə/ ....
7. /'mju:zɪk/ ....
8. /maɪ 'mʌðər ɪz dʒɜ:mən/ ....
....
9. /hə'ləʊ, aɪm 'dɪlən/ ....
....
10. /du: ju: laɪk tʃɒkəlɪt?/ ....
....
11. /ɑ: ju: 'gəʊɪn tu: 'saɪmənz 'pɑ:ti?/ ....
....

17 Transcris ces énoncés en phonétique.

1. chemist...
2. green shirt ....
3. We did not like the play...........................
4. She has been sick lately
....
5. He broke his glasses last week.
....
6. Have you seen my brother?
....
7. She liked reading when she was a child.
....

Bravo, tu es venu à bout de la partie Prononciation ! Il est maintenant temps de comptabiliser les icônes et de reporter le résultat en page 128 pour l'évaluation finale.

Culture et civilisation

Culture et civilisation

La fin de l'humour britannique ?

What would Great-Britain be without its legendary humour? As Oxford scholar[1] Theodore Zeldin once said: "the British have turned their sense of humour into a national virtue". A nice blend[2] of sarcasm, excentricity, irony, and self-deprecation[3], that's the unique recipe of British humour or so we have always been told. But recently some comedians like Dylan Moran or Eddie Izzard have called[4] that very old idea into question. English comedian Eddie Izzard – whose stand up comedy shows *Glorious*, *Dress to Kill*, and *Stripped* are world-famous[5] – even said that there was no British humour. To prove this, he has set himself[6] a gigantic task: he's been learning French, German, Spanish and is about to start with Arabian and Russian in order to perform[7] his stand up shows in these different countries. He has started with a French tour[8] that has been a great success. So, is it true that there is no real British humour after all? Maybe, let's see with a few Izzard samples[9]! Here we go:

- "I like my coffee like I like my women. In a plastic cup."
- "Racist people, interestingly, are never as polite as smokers. Have you noticed[10] that? Smokers always go, 'Do you mind[11] if I smoke? Oh, you do? Okay, I'll go outside and have a cigarette.' Racist people never go, 'Do you mind if I'm racist? Oh, I'll go outside and be racist'."

[1] *intellectuel*

[2] *mélange*

[3] *autodérision*

[4] **to call into question**, *remettre en question*

[5] *connus dans le monde entier*

[6] **to set oneself a task**, *se fixer un objectif*

[7] *se produire*

[8] *tournée*

[9] *échantillons*

[10] **to notice**, *remarquer*

[11] **to mind**, *être gêné par quelque chose*

I Right or Wrong ? Justifie tes réponses.

1. Theodore Zeldin is an Irish comedian. R - W ....

....

2. "Self-deprecation" means that you laugh at yourself. R - W ....

....

3. Dylan Moran is a comedian. R - W ....

....

4. *Glorious* is the name of a TV series. R - W ....

....

5. Izzard's shows are famous in Europe only. R - W ....

....

6. Izzard does not speak Russian yet. R - W ....

....

7. His tour in France has been successful. R - W ....

....

8. Izzard thinks smokers are rude. R - W ....

....

George VI

George VI was King of England from 1936 to 1952. He was not supposed to inherit[1] the Crown. His elder brother Edward VIIIth was. But he abdicated[2] in 1936 because he wanted to marry an American woman, who had divorced – she was named Wallis Simpson. George VI suffered from a speech impediment[3] called a stutter[4], which was a major problem for him because as a king, he often had to make speeches[5]. It was all the more[6] problematic as he lived at a time when people could listen to speeches on the radio. In 1925 – he was not king yet – he had to give a speech at the British Empire Exhibition in Wembley and could not utter[7] a word. After that incident, his wife looked for a good speech therapist to help him. All of that is shown in the 2010 film *The King's Speech*, with actor Colin Firth playing the role of the king. In this film you can see how a speech therapist called Lionel Logue helped him cure his stutter in order to enable[8] the King to make a very important speech on the radio in 1939, to declare war on[9] Germany. During WWII*, the King and his wife never left Buckingham Palace in spite of the Blitz – the massive German bombing plan to destroy Britain. During that dreadful[10] time they would visit people in the areas[11] that had been bombed to support them. Because of that, their memory is still much respected by English people today.

* World War 2 = The Second World War

[1] *hériter de*
[2] **to abdicate,** *abdiquer*
[3] *défaut d'élocution*
[4] *bégaiement*
[5] *discours*
[6] **all the more,** *d'autant plus*
[7] *prononcer*
[8] **permettre à,** *rendre possible*
[9] **to declare war on,** *déclarer la guerre à*
[10] *horrible*
[11] *zones*

Relie chaque indice à la bonne réponse (qui a besoin d'être complétée).

1. Type de spécialiste qui a aidé le roi	●	●	**a.** _ _lin F _ _ _ h
2. Année de la mort de George VI	●	●	**b.** s _ _ ec _ the_ _ pi _ _
3. Problème d'élocution de George VI	●	●	**c.** W_ll_s _ _mp_ _n
4. Joue le rôle de George VI dans un film	●	●	**d.** _ d_ar_ _lll
5. Nom des bombardements allemands sur Londres	●	●	**e.** nineteen ....- two
6. Nom du frère de George VI	●	●	**f.** a st _ _ _ er
7. Edouard VIII a épousé ...	●	●	**g.** _ embl_ _
8. Lieu de l'exposition impériale britannique en 1925	●	●	**h.** _ _ itz

Une figure historique féminine : Florence Nightingale

Florence Nightingale was born in Italy in 1820. She was a very curious and gifted[1] girl, who wanted to become a nurse. Her parents refused at first because a girl from a rich family was not supposed to work. But she was stubborn[2] and they finally let her go to Germany, where she got trained[3] for the job. When she came back to England in 1853, she ran[4] a hospital in London. But her nickname[5] comes from what happened next. In 1854, a war called *The Crimean War* started and she went to Turkey to take care of the wounded[6] soldiers. When she arrived there, she saw that most soldiers did not even die from the wounds they had but from diseases caused and spread[7] by a terrible lack of hygiene – like cholera, dysentry or typhus. She dramatically[8] improved hygiene and very soon fewer[9] soldiers died. Florence worked long hours and at night, she would visit the wounded holding[10] a lamp. That's why she was given the nickname *The Lady with the Lamp*. At the time people thought nurses did not have many skills[11] and it was not a respected job in England. Florence Nightingale changed people's point of view about it, showing that being a nurse required a lot of training and qualities.

[1] *douée*

[2] *têtue*

[3] *formée*

[4] **to run** (dans ce contexte), *diriger*

[5] *surnom*

[6] *blessés*

[7] **to spread**, *propager*

[8] *considérablement*

[9] **fewer** *est le comparatif de supériorité de* **few**

[10] **to hold**, *tenir*

[11] *compétences*

3 Complète les cases suivantes (mots en anglais).

1. Florence a été formée dans ce pays : ⬡⬡⬡⬡⬡⬡⬡
2. Elle y a dirigé un hôpital : ⬡⬡⬡⬡⬡⬡
3. Surnom de Florence : **The Lady with the** ⬡⬡⬡⬡
4. Pays de naissance de Florence : ⬡⬡⬡⬡⬡
5. Nom de la guerre qui éclate en 1854 : **The** ⬡⬡⬡⬡⬡⬡⬡ **War**
6. Profession de Florence : ⬡⬡⬡⬡⬡
7. Maladie qui se propage par manque d'hygiène : ⬡⬡⬡⬡⬡⬡⬡

Villes américaines

De nombreuses villes américaines ont des noms étranges, amusants, drôles et parfois franchement saugrenus ! Découvres-en quelques-uns :

NOMS COMMUNS
Chicken in Alaska
Rainbow in California
Pillow in Pennsylvania
Hammer in Dakota

Banque de mots
busy, *occupé*
colourful, *haut en couleurs*
comfort, *(ré)confort*
coward, *lâche, dégonflé*
darling, *chéri*
expected, *attendu*
eyebrow, *sourcil*
hammer, *marteau*

hell, *enfer*
hump, *bosse*
mean of transport, *moyen de transport*
pillow, *oreiller*
to rest, *se reposer*
rules, *règles*
twinned, *jumelé*
wise, *raisonnable, sage*

NOMS AMUSANTS
Monkey's Eyebrow in Kentucky
Camel Hump in Wyoming
Hungry Horse in Montana
Mexican Hat in Utah

TRAITS HUMAINS
Wise in Carolina
Busy in Kentucky
Uncertain in Texas
Coward in Carolina

NOTIONS GÉNÉRALES
Fair Play in California
Fidelity in Missouri
Simplicity in Virginia
Comfort in Texas

PAS ENGAGEANTS...
Badwater in California
Disappointment in Kentucky
Boring in Oregon
Hell in Michigan

PLUTÔT SYMPAS...
Darling in Mississippi
Welcome in California
Happy Land in Oklahoma
Smiley in Texas

HOTEL

4 Devine de quelle ville américaine il s'agit, en précisant l'État entre parenthèses.

1. This town has got so many things to do! .... (....................)

2. This town always respects the rules! .... (....................)

3. This town is not complicated! .... (....................)

4. You'd better drink soda there! .... (....................)

5. This town is not very interesting. .... (....................)

6. This is a ☺ town. .... (....................)

7. This town has a boyfriend/girlfriend sweet name. .... (....................)

8. This town is not as good as expected! .... (....................)

9. This town is colourful! .... (....................)

10. You rest your head on it. .... (....................)

11. May be twinned with Nail. .... (....................)

12. The cowboy's means of transport needs food. .... (....................)

Now, let's go to Scotland !

You bump into(1) someone you know, you're about to have to greet them but for a few seconds you cannot remember their name and your hesitation makes you feel super awkward(2). Has it ever happened to you? There is no word in the English language or in any language for that experience. Well, unless you're Scottish. The Scots have indeed a word for that unfortunate(3) momentary hesitation and the fact that you feel uncomfortable about it: it is called "to tartle". And if you want to apologise(4) for that to the person in question, you will say "Sorry for my tartle".

(1) **to bump into,** *tomber sur quelqu'un par hasard*

(2) *mal à l'aise*

(3) *regrettable*

(4) *s'excuser*

5  **Vrai ou Faux ? Justifie tes réponses.**

1. To tartle signifie juste oublier le nom de quelqu'un. V - F

....

2. To feel awkward signifie **to feel uncomfortable**. V - F

....

3. Le terme **tartle** ne s'utilise que comme verbe. V - F

....

6 **En t'appuyant sur les indices de la colonne de gauche, reconstitue le surnom de quelques villes britanniques.**

Indices

- La ville de **Manchester** a un climat océanique

- **Brighton** est une ville balnéaire du sud de l'Angleterre, à 50 minutes de Londres en train.

- "*Molly Malone*" est une célèbre chanson **irlandaise**, qui commence ainsi : "In ....'s fair city, where the girls are so pretty (...)"

- **Londres** a connu un grand problème de pollution dû à l'utilisation massive du charbon du XIXe siècle au milieu du xxe siècle. En 1905 un terme a été inventé pour désigner le type de pollution touchant cette ville : le **smog**, mélange de **fog** (brouillard) et de ....

- Édimbourg (**Edinburgh** en anglais) abrite de nombreux bâtiments publics de style grec néoclassique.

Réponses

London - sea - Athens - Rainy - Smoke - Fair

1. Edinburgh is the .... of the North.

2. .... by the .... is Brighton.

3. Manchester is the .... City.

4. London is the ....

5. Dublin is the .... City.

Molly Malone

Molly Malone, the woman

It is not a sure thing Molly Malone truly[1] existed as a real person. The legend says that she was a beautiful fishmonger[2] who lived in Dublin in the seventeenth century. At the time *Molly* was a nickname for *Mary*. Ireland's most famous song is about her and it is considered as the second Irish hymn. You'll hear it sung in pubs in Ireland but also in many English-speaking countries. A statue of Molly Malone was placed in Grafton Street in 1988, when the Dubliners celebrated the city's millenium.

The legend has a nasty[3] side[4] too. It says that Molly was a prostitute during the night, which is why she also has this not-so-nice nickname : the tart[5] with the cart[6].

[1] *vraiment*
[2] *poissonnière*
[3] *vilain*
[4] *aspect, côté*
[5] *pétasse*
[6] *chariot*
[7] *chariot, brouette*
[8] *coques et moules*
[9] *vivant*
[10] *fantôme*

Molly Malone, the song

In Dublin's fair city, where the girls are so pretty
I first set my eyes on sweet Molly Malone
As she wheeled her wheelbarrow[7]
Through streets broad and narrow
Crying cockles and mussels[8] alive a-live O!

A-live[9] a-live O! A-live a-live O!
Crying cockles and mussels alive a-live O!

She was a fishmonger and sure it was no wonder
For so were her father and mother before
And they both wheeled their barrows
Through streets broad and narrow
Crying cockles and mussels alive a-live O!

A-live a-live O! A-live a-live O!
Crying cockles and mussels alive a-live O!

She died of a fever and no one could save her
And that was the end of sweet Molly Malone
Now her ghost[10] wheels her barrow
Through streets broad and narrow

Crying cockles and mussels alive a-live O!

Vrai ou Faux ? Entoure la bonne réponse et corrige les affirmations fausses.

1. Molly est un surnom pour Mary. **V - F**

....

2. Molly Malone aurait vécu au
XIXᵉ siècle. **V - F**

....

3. Molly Malone est l'hymne irlandais.
V - F

....

4. Une statue de Molly a été installée sur
Grafton Street pour fêter les cent ans
de la ville. **V - F**

....

5. Molly aurait aussi vendu ses charmes
la nuit. **V - F**

....

6. Molly est morte de froid. **V - F**

....

7. Le fantôme de Molly hante les rues de
Dublin. **V - F**

....

8. set my eyes (ligne 2) signifie **saw**. **V - F**

....

9. Contrairement à leur fille, les parents
de Molly ne vendaient pas de poisson.
V - F

....

10. A-live a-live O! pourrait être traduit par
Il est frais mon poisson ! **V - F**

....

L'histoire de deux termes informatiques

Bug

Nowadays[1]*, computers are compact but there was a time when they would take a whole table! And sometimes, insects could get trapped[2] in them – In English, bug is an all-encompassing word[3] for insect by the way. The legend has it[4] that in 1945, a computer from Harvard University used by the American Army was making wrong calculations. The engineers looked inside to see what was wrong and they saw that some kind of butterfly[5] was stuck in it. They took the bug out, which gave birth[6] to the word *to debug*. It was not the only incident computers encountered with small animals because in a 1976 song called *The Little Mouse*, the singer Malvina Reynolds tells about a mouse who ate away the wires[7] on some computers at the Stock Exchange[8] and caused a moment of panic!

Bluetooth

Bluetooth is a technology which makes communication possible between devices[9] at small distances. It was created by the Swedish company Ericsson. Why is it called *Bluetooth*? Well, apparently the technology was named after Danish[10] King Harald Bluetooth, who united Denmark and Norway[11] in the tenth century.

*Traductions en haut de la page suivante

(1) *de nos jours*

(2) *piégés*

(3) **all-encompassing word,** *terme général*

(4) **the legend has it,** *selon*

la légende

(5) *papillon*

(6) **to give birth to,** *donner naissance à*

(7) *fils électriques*

(8) **Stock Exchange,** *Bourse*

(9) *appareils*

(10) *danois*

(11) *Norvège*

 Vrai ou Faux ?

1. À l'origine le mot **bug** signifie papillon en anglais. V - F

2. Le mot *débugger* est un terme venant de la Bourse. V - F

3. Dans la chanson de Malvina Reynolds, la petite souris s'attaque aux ordinateurs de l'armée américaine. V - F

4. Le Bluetooth est une technologie d'origine danoise. V - F

5. *Ericsson* est le nom de l'entreprise qui a inventé le Bluetooth. V - F

Découvrons ensemble l'influence de Shakespeare sur l'anglais d'aujourd'hui

La langue anglaise doit beaucoup au célèbre dramaturge puisqu'il serait à l'origine de 3 000 nouveaux mots, dont certains sont devenus très banals comme **bedroom, luggage, label** (*étiquette*), **elbow** (*coude*) ou encore l'expression **fair-play.**

Banque de mots

to get rid of, *se débarrasser de*

kingdom, *royaume*

madness, *folie*

pickle, *cornichon*

rotten, *pourri*

stitch, *point (de suture)*

suddenly, *soudain*

 Que peuvent bien signifier ces expressions courantes venant de Shakespeare ?

1. **a sea change** est :
   a. une tempête
   b. un changement radical

2. **all of a sudden** signifie :
   a. tout d'un coup
   b. en même temps

3. **good riddance!** signifie :
   a. bon débarras
   b. bonne chance

4. **to be in a pickle** signifie :
   a. être acide
   b. être dans de beaux draps !

5. **to be in stitches** signifie :
   a. être mort de rire
   b. être très en retard

Certaines phrases de Shakespeare sont encore employées aujourd'hui dans certains contextes. Découvrons-en trois ensemble :

1. **Something is rotten in the state of Denmark.**
2. **There's method in my madness.**
3. **My kingdom for a horse!**

 À ton avis, laquelle utilise-t-on...

a. ... quand on désire une chose toute simple mais inestimable dans le contexte présent (ex. : un simple verre d'eau quand on a très soif) ?

....

b. ... quand il y a quelque chose de suspect.

....

c. ... pour dire qu'il y a toujours une explication à un comportement.

....

L'anglais est riche d'expressions formées par des paires de noms séparés par une conjonction (généralement **and** ou **or**, ex. : **neat and tidy,** *très bien rangé*). Il existe souvent (mais pas tout le temps) un jeu sur les sonorités entre les deux termes (ex. : **to be part and parcel,** *être partie intégrante, indissociable*).

En utilisant tes connaissances acquises et ta logique, essaie de reconstituer quelques expressions en plaçant l'un des mots fournis au bon endroit.

break, safe, fair, live, tired

Expressions	Signification
1. .... **and square**	*de manière tout à fait honnête*
2. **(to be) sick and**	*en avoir par-dessus la tête !*
3. .... **and sound**	*sain et sauf !*
4. **make or**..................	*ça passe ou ça casse !*
5. .... **and learn**	dicton signifiant que la vie donne de l'expérience

Banque de mots

from what you're saying,
d'après ce que tu dis

to hang about,
traîner ensemble

12 Découvrons ensemble quelques expressions idiomatiques ! À partir de la conversation que Tom a avec son père, essaie de déduire le sens des expressions soulignées.

Father	→ You seem preoccupied. <u>A penny for your thoughts</u>?
Tom	→ I wonder if I should go to Patrick's party. We no longer hang about as we used to. We see each other <u>once in a blue moon</u> now. And I don't really like him anymore.
Father	→ Well, from what you're saying, it's a <u>no-brainer</u> then. Don't go. So... I can see you're <u>burning the midnight oil</u>.
Tom	→ Not really, I'm just playing this new video game.
Father	→ I know... I was saying that <u>tongue in cheek</u>. I can see that you're not studying for your test tomorrow!

1. A penny for your thoughts?	2. Once in a blue moon	3. A no-brainer	4. Tongue in cheek	5. To burn the midnight oil
a. *shut up!*	a. *during the night*	a. *a difficult decision*	a. *seriously*	a. *to cook*
b. *what are you thinking about?*	b. *rarely*	b. *an easy decision*	b. *quickly*	b. *to smoke*
c. *why are you laughing?*	c. *all the time*	c. *a stupid person*	c. *ironically*	c. *to work late*

Finissons ce cahier avec quelques exercices pour se familiariser avec l'argot !

13 En t'appuyant sur ce petit dialogue entre Kyle et Darren, essaie de déduire le sens des mots soulignés (attribue le numéro de chaque expression dans les parenthèses prévues à cet effet).

Kyle	→ **Hey <u>mate</u> ( )**
Darren	→ **What's up?**
Kyle	→ **I'm <u>knackered</u> ( ), I was up all night, mate! Didn't see ya at the concert last night, it was <u>savage</u> ( )!**
Darren	→ **I know, I'm <u>gutted</u> ( ). My parents <u>went ballistic</u> ( ) when they heard we were going with Jake. They don't want me to hang out with him, they say he's a <u>chav</u> ( ).**
Kyle	→ **<u>It sucks</u> ( )! Jake is not a chav. He's just a <u>weirdo</u> ( ).**
Darren	→ **I know, I told them, I'm so <u>pissed off</u> ( ). Wanna buy some <u>fags</u> ( ), d'ya have a <u>buck</u> ( )?**
Kyle	→ **nah, I'm <u>broke</u> ( ) man. Fuck, I need the <u>bog</u> ( ), I'm gonna <u>barf</u> ( ). I knew this kebab was fishy** *(suspect, louche)*!

1. un dollar

2. ça craint

3. mon pote

4. péter un câble

5. fauché

6. une caillera (racaille)

7. les chiottes

8. chelou (bizarre)

9. dégueuler

10. à cran, énervé

11. dégoûté (dans le sens *super déçu*)

12. crevé

13. mortel ! (super, génial)

14. clopes

14 Remplace la forme familière en gras par la forme plus soutenue.

1. How are **ya?**..

2. I'm running **cuz** I'm late. ....

3. I **dunno** where she is. ....

4. **Gimme** that book. ....

5. I'm **gonna** eat. ....

6. She doesn't **wanna** see me. ....

7. **Watcha** doing?...

8. There's **lotsa** work to do. ....

9. Get **outta** here! ....

Le cas de *ain't*

Ain't est un terme argotique grammaticalement incorrect, qui peut signifier plusieurs choses (selon le contexte). Il existe un proverbe disant **If it ain't broken, don't fix i**t (*On ne répare pas quelque chose qui n'est pas cassé*).

15 Devine les différents sens de **ain't**.

1. She ain't sleeping. ....

2. I ain't gonna help ya. ....

3. They ain't seen it. ....

4. He ain't got wheels. ....

Bravo, tu es venu à bout de la partie Culture et civilisation ! Il est maintenant temps de comptabiliser les icônes et de reporter le résultat en page 128 pour l'évaluation finale.

Verbes irréguliers

Infinitif	Prétérit	Participe passé	Traduction
be	was/were	been	*être*
begin	began	begun	*commencer*
bite	bit	bitten	*mordre*
break	broke	broken	*casser*
build	built	built	*construire*
buy	bought	bought	*acheter*
catch	caught	caught	*attraper*
come	came	come	*venir*
cost	cost	cost	*coûter*
draw	drew	drawn	*dessiner*
dream	dreamt	dreamt	*rêver*
drink	drank	drunk	*boire*
eat	ate	eaten	*manger*
fall	fell	fallen	*tomber*
feel	felt	felt	*(se) sentir*
fight	fought	fought	*combattre*
forbid	forbade	forbidden	*interdire*
forget	forgot	forgotten	*oublier*
get	got	got	*obtenir*
give	gave	given	*donner*
go	went	gone	*aller*
have	had	had	*avoir*
hear	heard	heard	*entendre*
know	knew	known	*savoir, connaître*
learn	learnt	learnt	*apprendre*
leave	left	left	*partir, quitter*
lend	lent	lent	*prêter*
make	made	made	*faire, fabriquer*
meet	met	met	*(se) rencontrer*
read	read	read	*lire*
run	ran	run	*courir*
say	said	said	*dire*
see	saw	seen	*voir*
sell	sold	sold	*vendre*
send	sent	sent	*envoyer*
sing	sang	sung	*chanter*
sleep	slept	slept	*dormir*
speak	spoke	spoken	*parler*
spend	spent	spent	*dépenser*
steal	stole	stolen	*voler*
take	took	taken	*prendre*
teach	taught	taught	*enseigner*
tell	told	told	*dire, raconter*
win	won	won	*gagner*
write	wrote	written	*écrire*

SOLUTIONS

GRAMMAIRE
Unité 1

1 dairy/meat/shrimp/grapes/plum/waffle/corn/pear/ham/honey/oil/mushroom/peach/grapefruit/leek
1. grapes **2.** shrimp **3.** pear **4.** oil **5.** mushroom **6.** dairy **7.** leek **8.** waffle

2 **1.** is **2.** are **3.** Is **4.** is **5.** is. **6.** are **7.** are. **8.** is **9.** are. **10.** is. **11.** is/are **12.** are

3 **1.** There's a mouse in the cellar. **2.** correct **3.** I would like Ø/the/some honey. **4.** She's writing on Ø/the/a piece of paper. **5.** correct **6.** I'm drinking Ø/the/some/a glass of (= un verre de) water. **7.** Your pyjamas are dirty. **8.** The team are ready for the game.

4 **vegetables:** mashed potatoes, chips, lettuce, French beans, asparagus - **fruit:** cherry, grapefruit, apricot, peach, watermelon, strawberrry - **cereals:** rice, pasta - **meat:** lamb, ham - **seafood:** salmon, tuna - **condiments:** honey, pepper

5 **1.** some - any **2.** any - some **3.** any **4.** any **5.** many **6.** much **7.** much **8.** many **9.** much **10.** many

6 **1.** any - a little **2.** much **3.** many **4.** a little, every **5.** few, enough **6.** too much - any **7.** no - little **8.** how much

7

8 **1. g.** brush your teeth **2. c.** fall asleep **3. e.** fly **4. h.** hang about **5. f.** wear **6. b.** take a bath **7. a.** take the underground **8. d.** shave

9 **1.** It means **2.** is wearing **3.** correct **4.** wants **5.** What does your father do? **6.** What are you doing? **7.** do you go

10 **1.** diary **2.** abroad - in the country **3.** cello **4.** jewel **5.** tie

11 **1.** hang about **2.** is living **3.** not eating **4.** stands. **5.** walk **6.** eat – I'm eating **7.** Do you believe in… ?

12 **A.** He hardly ever has a waffle. **2.** He seldom has fruit (apricots). **3.** He has crisps once a week. **4.** He usually has chocolate.

13 **1.** can't stand **2.** is crazy about/digs – favourite **3.** all the same to her – dislikes/loathes **4.** shrimps **5.** Harriet **6.** shrimps **7.** yuck

14

15 **1.** either - or - neither - nor **2.** neither - nor - either - or

16 **1.** Roger prefers bitter flavours to sweet flavours **2.** My little brother prefers crosswords to jigsaw puzzles. **3.** Your little sister prefers fairy tales to jigsaw puzzles. **4.** My mother prefers poetry to detective stories.

17 **1.** rock climbing **2.** coin collecting **3.** bird watching **4.** kart racing **5.** ice skating

18 **1.** He doesn't mind taking the bin out. **2.** He hates dusting. **3.** He enjoys ironing. **4.** Ironing **5.** He prefers ironing to dusting.

19 **1.** How about/what about singing in a choir? **2.** How about/what about playing drums in a band? **3.** How about/what about learning cello?

20 **1. b.** She's keen on sculpting. **2. g.** He's crazy about bowling. **3. e.** He's afraid of paintball. **4. a.** She prefers hiking to knitting. **6. d.** He's interested in scubadiving. **7. h.** I can't bear mountain biking. **8. f.** We're fed up with hiking.

21 **1.** wearing a tie is a good idea **2.** Not sharing her snack is not nice

22 **1.** … for three weeks **2.** … since 2005 **3.** … been a nurse? **4.** … spent … **5.** I have been waiting …

23 **1.** has been divorced **2.** have been cleaning **3.** have been waiting **4.** have you played **5.** has been eating **6.** have seen

24 **1.** since **2.** for **3.** since **4.** for **5.** since

25 **1.** Anna has been studying a lot lately. - **b.** - Anna étudie beaucoup dernièrement. **2.** We have been running for an hour. - **a.** - Nous courons depuis une heure. **3.** How long have they been arguing? - **c.** - Depuis combien de temps se disputent-ils ?

26 **1.** Do you know Simon's step-father? What does he do? **2.** She's always using my game console! **3.** I always fall asleep at midnight. **4.** Your neighbour has been weak since his accident. **5.** How long have you been writing a diary? **6.** We seldom take the underground. **7.** How often do you take it? Twice a month **8.** Mrs Sanders hardly ever wears jewels but today she's wearing a necklace. **9.** What is your sister doing ? She's playing the cello. **10.** My parents have been married for twenty years. **11.** The air contains oxygene. **12.** I have been sleeping a lot lately.

27 **1.** customers' rights. **2.** Men's Health. **3.** Karim's and Nora's fathers (il ne s'agit pas ici d'un père en commun, ils ont chacun le leur!) **4.** to the hairdresser's **5.** Oliver's **6.** our mice's cheese. **7.** the neighbours' daughter. **8.** to the butcher's **9.** Helen and Gabriel's mother (ici la mère est en commun, la marque de possession ne porte donc que sur Gabriel) **10.** James's fault

28 **1.** her – ours **2.** Their - Yours **3.** mine

29 **1.** hers – belongs **2.** owner - his

30 **1.a.** R **b.** W, she's got two brothers and sisters **c.** W, she's (growing) old - **2. a.** R **b.** W, he's an only child **c.** R **d.** W, he's middle-aged - **3.a.** W, he's married **b.** W, he's got one brother or sister **c.** W, he's young

31 **1.** married **2.** widower **3.** He's got no job **4.** an only child **5.** bald **6.** husband **7.** (growing) old **8.** middle-aged

32 **1.** Jean **2.** Louis **3.** Julien

33 **1.** plump **2.** skinny **3.** neither beautiful nor ugly.

34 Eric is/looks clumsy **(1)**, grumpy **(5)**, and thoughtful **(8)** - Simon is/looks funny **(2)**, helpful **(4)**, quiet **(7)** and cheerful **(10)** - Tommy is/looks selfish **(3)**, lazy **(6)**, and shy **(9)**

35 1. messy – filthy 2. shabby 3. dirty 4. cluttered 5. dusty 6. neat and tidy 7. cramped - cosy

36 1. alone – lonely 2. ill – sick 3. scared – afraid 4. alive - living

37 1. A dead man – the living 2. Pole – The Polish 3. Young men – the retired 4. The French – Frenchmen 5. an Irishman – The Irish 6. Spanish – Spaniard

38 1. frightened 2. amazing 3. annoying 4. annoyed 5. frightening 6. amazed

39 A. 1. e (well-known) 2. i (homesick) 3. g (life-changing) 4. j (animal-shaped) 5. a (left-handed) 6. b (open-minded) 7. d (part-time) 8. h (old-fashioned) 9. c (long-haired) 10. f (two-year old) - B. 1. animal 2. minded 3. life 4. old 5. home 6. known 7. long-haired 8. two-year old 9. left-handed 10. part-time

40 1. an ugly small brown German dog 2. a magnificent huge medieval Scottish castle 3. an old-fashioned tall ninety-year-old Spanish man

41 1. frying-pan 2. chatterbox (*pipelette*) 3. redhead (*rouquine*) 4. ice cream (*glace*) 5. housework (*tâches ménagères*) 6. keyhole (*serrure*) 7. haircut (*coupe de cheveux*)

42 1. paper 2. pill 3. shaving 4. cleaning 5. stick 6. pool 7. machine 8. case

43 1. b 2. d 3. e 4. a 5. f 6. c

44 1. What disgusting pasta! 2. How cosy that room is! 3. Your father is such a good-looking man! 4. How cute their freckles are! 5. These strawberries are so sweet! 6. What a cool hoodie he's wearing!

45 1. the – Ø 2. Ø – the 3. a – an 4. Ø – Ø - Ø 5. an – a – a 6. the – Ø 7. Ø - Ø 8. a 9. Ø - the. 10. Ø 11. Ø – a

Unité 2

1 1. b 2. a 3. a 4. c 5. b

2 1. I will buy a new car when I get a better job. (a) 2. We are about to start dinner. (e) 3. Eric is dumping his girlfriend tonight. (d) 4. I will lend you some money. (g) 5. Our president visits the factory tomorrow. (c) 6. I'll come with you! (f) 7. She looks very sad, she's going to cry. (b)

3 1. Samuel is sick but he's not going to die. 2. Anna is yawning, she's going to fall asleep. 3. My father is taking his razor, he's going to shave. 4. Clara is pregnant, she's going to have a baby. 5. Ian and Sofia are engaged, they're going to get married. 6. You are going to apologise.

4 1. begins 2. will make – are 3. is about to 4. 'm going to call 5. will tell 6. get.

5 1. be +ing (prévu) 2. will (volonté) 3. be +ing (prévu) 4. will (volonté)

6 1. will forgive 2. is proposing 3. is quitting 4. She will 5. will get

7 1. I'll be driving my new car 2. I'll be living in my new house 3. We will be running the marathon

8 1. When/What time does the Shakespeare play begin? 2. How long are you going to live abroad? 3. Why will you not/won't you sing? 4. Who will be working with us tomorrow?

9 1. I hope you recover soon. 2. I will buy a new computer if we save enough money. 3. I will not hoover. 4. When I am big, I will be a lawyer. 5. Does the film start at nine p.m.? 6. In a week (from now), you will be swimming in Greece.

10 1. k 2. g 3. j 4. a 5. h 6. b 7. d 8. c 9. f 10. i 11. e

11 1. c 2. c 3. b 4. b 5. a

12 1. disabled 2. can't hear 3. can't see. 4. dumb

13 1. stand - *Je ne supporte pas les gens qui sont toujours en retard.* 2. help - *Mon frère ne peut pas s'empêcher de se ronger les ongles.* 3. be bothered - *Elle a la flemme de répondre au téléphone.* 4. wait - *Ils ont hâte de te voir la semaine prochaine.* 5. enough - *Je ne me lasse jamais des pâtes.*

14 1. My husband can have a bad temper sometimes. 2. You must be very depressed. 3. You must rent a cheaper flat. 4. Will you be allowed to leave earlier? 5. It can't be easy for you. 6. You mustn't lie. 7. I can't hang about with my friends today. 8. They don't have to take the underground. 9. They're not able to solve that problem. 10. You can become a lawyer if you work hard. 11. May I borrow your laptop? 12. Winter can be very cold in Canada. 13. I will have to tell the truth to the police. 14. Will they be able to arrive on time? 15. She can't cook very well. 16. You may play video games if you do your homework.

a. 6 b. 7, 9, 15 c. 8 d. 16 e. 4, 11 f. 10, 14 g. 2

15 1. can 2. must – have to 3. must 4. will be able to 5. can't 6. can't – mustn't – are not allowed to 7. can't - don't have to 8. must 9. can't

16 1. You can't hear the neighbour sing. 2. It can't be getting late now. 3. You must/have to call me. 4. Is she able to hike long distances? 5. Is she allowed to run again? 6. I may not introduce you to my wife.

17 1. I won't be able to save much money. 2. They will have to stop biting their nails. 3. You won't be allowed to smoke in my house.

18 1. must 2. has to 3. must 4. have to

19 1. doesn't need 2. needn't 3. don't need 4. needn't

20 1. When/what time do you have to go to bed in boarding schools? 2. What needn't we bring? 3. Why must you help your sister? 4. Who can sometimes be rude?

21 1. She may not go out. 2. They must be playing rugby. 3. He can work hard. 4. It can't be his fault. 5. You must get up. 6. Need I take a coat?

22 1. Will you be able to be on time? 2. You needn't cancel the appointment. I will do it. 3. I can't help being disappointed. 4. He must be sleeping. 5. My neighbour is deaf and dumb. But he can see. 6. You have to follow the rules when you play rugby. It's compulsory. 7. I must go back home earlier tonight. My father needs me.

23

1. travel 2. share 3. spend 4. order 5. forgive 6. apologise 7. exercise 8. rest 9. socialize 10. fail

24

25 1. He would like to be a computer programmer. *Il voudrait être programmeur informatique.* 2. I would rather not go to bed too late tonight. *Je préférerais ne pas me coucher trop tard ce soir.* 3. Could you water the flowers, please? *Pourrais-tu/Pourriez-vous arroser les fleurs, s'il te/vous plaît ?* 4. Shall we go to the party together? *Et si on allait à la fête ensemble ?* 5. Does she prefer to rest or to socialize? *Est-ce qu'elle préfère se reposer ou sortir/voir des gens ?*

26 1. I would like to make a reservation - I would rather make a reservation 2. They would like to travel more - They would rather travel more 3. Would she like to buy a return ticket to Leeds? - Would she rather buy a return ticket to Leeds?

27 1. prefer – shall we have 2. prefer – would rather. 3. would rather 4. shall we go - would you rather 5. prefer – shall we go

28 1. Could you not smoke in the house? 2. Could you give me a hand?

29 1. We'd like to spend our holidays in Japan. Shall we go together? 2. Would you like to order, Sir? 3. The apple pie doesn't look good. She would rather have the vanilla ice cream. 4. I generally prefer to take the underground but tonight I would rather take the bus. Shall we share a cab? 5. Could you give me a hand?

30 1. correct 2. You ought to respect the highway code. 3. We had better not spend so much money. 4. She should go to the hairdresser's. 5. You ought to switch off your phone in hospitals. 6. correct

31 1. She had better save some money but she would rather spend it during the sales.

32 1. She should/'d better rest but she'd rather travel a lot. 2. She should/'d better do the laundry but she'd rather walk her dog.

33 1. Had we better get some sleep? - We'd better not get some sleep. 2. Had they rather tell him? - They'd rather not tell him.

34 Anna feels dizzy : 3 - Jim is eating with his fingers : 2 - David is very lonely : 6 - Liam has got a bad report : 4 - John says « silly cop » : 5 - Kelly doesn't know what to do : 1

35 1. You'd better study more or you'll fail your exam. 2. You'd better not forget your coat or you'll be cold.

36 1. You'd better not chat with strangers online. 2. You ought to pay your taxes. 3. Your nose is running. Maybe you should blow it.

37 classement : Henry – Eric – Lucy – Adam - 1. Eric 3. Adam

38 1. she might be hiking 2. She must be in a good mood 3. They may go on strike 4. She should be relieved now

39 1. She may burst into tears when you tell her the news. 2. She passed her exam yesterday, she must be so relieved!

40 1. against 2. above 3. across 4. through

41 1. next to – *Pourriez-vous vous asseoir/pourrais-tu t'asseoir à côté de moi ?* 2. far away – *Je préférerais ne pas vivre loin de mes amis.* 3. behind – *Au Japon, les épouses devraient marcher derrière leur mari.* 4. between – *Je ferais mieux de m'asseoir entre Ian et Jane, ils se disputent tout le temps !*

42 1. His/her flat may be opposite the station. 2. Can you jump over the wall? 3. Children should stay away from the fire and should not run around the swimming pool. 4. Tomorrow, we will be walking along the beach.

Unité 3

1 1. a 2. b 3. c 4. a 5. a 6. c

2 1. was/wasn't – were 2. Were 3. wasn't 4. were 5. were 6. weren't

3 1. correct 2. bited : bit 3. eated : ate 4. costed : cost 5. catched : caught 6. learned : learnt 7. forbided : forbade 8. correct 9. breaked : broke 10. readed : read

4 1. worked 2. broke 3. Did your husband retire 4. gave 5. Did they sing

5 1. Mr Anderson taught English when he was young. 2. My parents sold our house last year. 3. She didn't meet the President yesterday. 4. The company cancelled our flight an hour ago. 5. Did they intend to move out? 6. I wrote a poem for you last week.

6 1. I didn't see Anna at the station yesterday. 2. You left your umbrella at home. 3. Did we sleep for ten hours last night? 4. They drank some alcohol at the party. 5. Were you spending your holidays abroad? 6. Would I travel less if I had children?

7 1. was cheating - scolded me. 2. was not running – sprained – was walking 3. knew – forgot 4. were 5. were 6. stole

8 1. What were you doing when I/we called? 2. What would you do if you were my mother? 3. When did she buy this new computer? 4. What did your mother do from 1980 to 2000? 5. Where were they going when the accident happened?

9 1. I had some time yesterday, so I was able to help you. 2. She felt sick a few hours ago and she had to stay home. 3. When I was a child, I could not swim well. 4. Why did she have to come over when I was sick? 5. In 1960, workers were not allowed to retire at 60.

10 1. d 2. c 3. f 4. e 5. b 6. a 7. i 8. k 9. h 10. l 11. j 12. g

11 1. I used to go to painting exhibitions – I don't go to painting exhibitions any more. 2. We used to sing in a choir – We no longer sing in a choir.

12 1. We used to go to work by bus but we no longer do. 2. My mother used to drink a lot of coffee but she no longer does. 3. Did they use to like painting exhibitions? No, they didn't use to. They used to prefer hiking. 4. Did the Jones use to scold their children? No, they didn't use to. They used to spoil them a lot. 5. We used to have no car but we bought one last year.

13 1. Were you exercising when I came over? 2. We bumped into Emma at the market two days ago. 3. I used to go to the cinema every Friday (but I no longer do). 4. We would go to the restaurant together. 5. We didn't go to the museum last week. 6. If I were you I would not scold the children. 7. Would her husband be handsome if he had a beard?

14 1. made it yourself 2. did it himself 3. bought one ourselves 4. herself 5. themselves 6. myself

15 1. He looked at himself in the mirror and found himself old. 2. She's not nice. We realised that this morning. 3. We took good care of ourselves.

16 1. introduced herself 2. killed himself 3. got dressed 4. enjoyed ourselves 5. relaxed Ø 6. hurried up Ø

17 1. I have forgotten to buy stamps 2. Have you ever seen a UFO? 3. correct 4. Have they taken a shower yet? 5. We have never eaten snails. 6. He hasn't begun his homework yet.

18 1. Have you forgotten these old shoes in the cellar? 2. He hasn't begun repainting the ceiling.

19 1. never 2. ever 3. already 4. just 5. yet

20 1. Yes, they've already been afraid of blood. 2. No, I've never wanted to live in the 18th century.

21 1. Have you ever seen the President? Yes, I saw him this morning. 2. Has she ever tried Swedish food? Yes, she tried it yesterday. 3. Has he ever bought a scooter? Yes, he bought one two days ago.

22 1. e. He has never read Harry Potter. 2. c The fridge is empty. 3. a He's had a serious car accident. 4. d He's not single anymore. 5. b. Do you know if she's ok?

23 1. so 2. because 3. so 4. because

24 1. We haven't seen the exhibition yet. 2. I have missed a step, I've got bruises. 3. My sister has just caught a cold. She coughed all night. 4. Have you ever been married? 5. She has never scolded her children. 6. Have you seen the remote control?

25 1. She's slept better since she decided to take sleeping pills. 2. He's been nicer since he got married.

26 1. It has been two days since I smoked a cigar (cela fait deux jours que j'ai fumé un cigare), I haven't smoked a cigar for two days (je n'ai pas fumé de cigare depuis deux jours) 2. I has been a year since we went to the doctor's (cela fait un an que nous sommes allés chez le médecin), We haven't been to the doctor's for a year (nous ne sommes pas allés chez le médecin depuis un an)

27 1. How many times have you seen this film? 2. How long have you slept?

28 1. It's the sweetest apple she's ever eaten. 2. It's the least expensive/the cheapest necklace I have ever bought. 3. It's the messiest flat he has ever lived in. 4. Vaccines are the most important discovery doctors have ever seen. 5. That is the worst film I have ever seen !

29 1. each other 2. one another 3. Ø 4. one another 5. Ø

30 1. probabilité haute 2. reproche 3. regret 4. probabilité moyenne 5. suggestion 6. reproche

31 1. He must have been sick. 2. She might have eaten less. 3. I should have studied harder. 4. He may have been hungry.

32 1. b, d   2. a, c

33 1. You've been eating chocolate again! 2. We have eaten all the chocolate.

34 1. a, d   2. b, e   3. c, f

35 It has been raining – It has been snowing

36 1. had been cleaning – offered 2. had already had – invited 3. had you ever been - went 4. had been feeling sick – recovered

37 1. I had already met Adam when you introduced us to each other. – J'avais déjà rencontré Adam quand tu nous as présentés (l'un à l'autre). 2. I fell asleep before the film started. – Je me suis endormi avant le début du film.

38 1. He had been eating for five minutes when he broke a tooth. 2. We had been singing in the same choir for a year when we fell in love.

39 1. I wish you had come to my party – If only you had come to my party. – Si seulement tu étais venu à ma fête. 2. She wishes she had not eaten this fish – If only she had not eaten this fish. – Si seulement elle n'avait pas mangé ce poisson.

40 1. I had seen the exhibition when it ended. 2. They had been married for five years when she got pregnant. 3. You had already bought a ticket when the concert was cancelled. 4. If only I had been nicer to him. – I wish I had been nicer to him.

Unité 4

1 1. isn't he? 2. can you? 3. shall we? 4. are they? 5. didn't you? 6. aren't I?

7. has it? 8. do you? 9. will you? 10. won't he ? 11. has she? 12. was it?

2 1. So did they. 2. Neither have I. 3. Neither can Lana. 4. So does my sister. 5. So has their daughter.

3 1. You sister is always complaining, isn't she? (l'utilisation du présent be +-ing marque ici l'énervement). 2. My girlfriend is in a good mood. So is her brother. 3. She hasn't missed the bus, has she?

4 1. from 2. with 3. in 4. to 5. for

5 1. depend on the weather 2. suffered from headaches 3. wait for me 4. deals with

6 1. What will your choice depend on? 2. What are you interested in? 3. What does he suffer from?

7 1. refuser 2. arrêter/abandonner 3. tomber sur quelque chose (par hasard) 4. être à court de 5. tomber en panne

8 1. She is making a pizza. 2. I made a pizza. 3. They have made a pizza. 4. We had made a pizza. 5. She would make a pizza.

9 1. are killed 2. was invented 3. will be opened 4. is spoken 5. is being eaten 6. had just been married 7. had (already) been mugged – was being mugged

10 1. A new planet will be discovered by Professor Moonlight. Voix active: Professor Moonlight will discover a new planet. 2. This film has not been subtitled by our teacher. Voix active : Our teacher has not subtitled this film.

11 1. A new treatment has been discovered. 2. A beautiful piece of furniture was given to us. – We were given a beautiful piece of furniture.

12 1. A strange e-mail has been sent to me. 2. A lie was told to us. 3. They will be bought a large house. 4. She is being given a lot of free time.

13 1. is being written 2. will be told 3. was promised 4. has been taught

14 1. Eggs are given to us by the farmer every week. We are given eggs by the farmer every week. 2. An assignment has been given to us by the history teacher. We have been given an assignment by the history teacher.

15 1. d. "I don't like cinnamon." 2. f. "I'm going to marry Helena soon." 3. e. "Go do your homework!" 4. c. "He went shopping there yesterday." 5. b. "My wife has been ill for 5 years." **6. a.** « She/he/they can borrow our car."

16 1. She says that her ex boyfriend had prejudices **2.** He said that he had been living in France for 10 years. **3.** She said that you must not disturb her son. **4.** He said that they would go to the opera the day after. **5.** He told me to help my mother with the cooking the following week. **6.** She said that she was in love with me/him.

17 1. Tell me what your astrological sign is. **2.** I wonder if/whether he wants to dump her. **3.** I asked him/her how tall his/her brother was. **4.** Do you know where my glasses are? **5.** He told me not to ask too many questions.

18 1. "When will they visit?" **2.** "Have they/has she/he been warned or not?" **3.** "May I smoke?" **4.** "Don't tell your sister!"

19 1. Your brother told me that you had been divorced since 2008. **2.** We don't know what 'swag' means. **3.** They asked me not to warn you.

20 1. opium dens **2.** a factory **3.** drinking water **4.** a bachelor **5.** washing powder **6.** a cleaning lady

21 1. that/Ø – who **2.** where **3.** which **4.** that **5.** what **6.** which/that/Ø **7.** whose **8.** when

22 1. I have not put on weight, which is a good thing. – *Je n'ai pas pris de poids, ce qui est une bonne chose.* **2.** The epidemy happened in the 15th century, when people had no drinking water. – *L'épidémie a eu lieu au 15e siècle, à une époque où les gens ne disposaient pas d'eau potable.* **3.** The accident happened in the factory where my father used to work. – *L'accident a eu lieu dans l'usine où mon père travaillait.* **4.** I take classes with a skiing instructor whose eyes are the most beautiful ever. *Je prends des cours avec un moniteur de ski dont les yeux sont les plus beaux qui soient !* **5.** You bought some washing powder that/which smells good. – *Tu as acheté une lessive qui sent bon.* ou The washing powder which/that/Ø you bought smells good. – *La lessive que tu as achetée sent bon.* **6.** I don't care what you think about me. – *Je me fiche de ce que tu penses de moi.*

23 1. as long as **2.** whereas **3.** in order to **4.** in spite of **5.** however **6.** but

24 1. unless – *Tu n'auras pas l'autorisation de quitter le travail plus tôt, à moins que ton manager ne soit d'accord.* **2.** yet – *Il mange comme deux. Et pourtant*

il est très mince ! **3.** As – *Vu que j'étais dans le quartier, j'ai décidé de passer.* **4.** If – *Si tu me dis quel est le problème, je pourrais peut-être t'aider.* **5.** Although – *Bien qu'elle ait très bien conduit, elle a échoué à son examen de permis de conduire.*

25 1. We tried to call her but she did not pick up. **2.** I did all my homework on Friday so as to be rid of it for the week end. **3.** I don't regret helping her, even though she didn't even thank me.

26 1. Unlike Mia, her sister isn't fluent in English. – Mia is fluent in English, unlike her sister **2.** I run twice a week, whereas brother doesn't. – My brother doesn't run, whereas I do.

27 1. I got up at sunrise in order to/to go for a run. **2.** He (has) stopped by in spite of the snow. **3.** If the architect and the accountant do not agree to it, the advertising campaign will not happen / will not take place. **4.** As/since your wall is damaged, you're going to need a bricklayer, not a chemist! **5.** Unlike you, I (have) failed my driving test.

28 1. tell him? **2.** telling him **3.** to tell him **4.** tell him? **5.** telling him **6.** to tell him **7.** telling him **8.** tell him **9.** telling him **10.** telling him

29 1. needs cutting **2.** helped him write **3.** correct **4.** We did not expect you to arrive so early. **5.** Instead of whining – help me repair **6.** hear her gossip/gossiping

30 1. The teacher wants us to be more focused in class. **2.** Could you help me wrap up the Christmas presents? **3.** I made the cleaning lady hoover. **4.** You must write this application letter without making any mistakes. **5.** Sarah's parents would like her to whine less. **6.** It's no use crying over spilt milk.

31 1. I don't mind wrapping up the presents. Remember to buy some bread! **2.** Arrête de te plaindre et concentre-toi ! **3.** Je ne m'attendais pas à ce qu'elle fasse des commérages comme ça! **4.** Taking a glass of milk before going to bed will help you relax. **5.** Your hair needed washing! **6.** Can you help me repair/fix my computer? **7.** Nous étions occupés à rédiger une lettre de candidature. **8.** Cela ne sert à rien de pleurnicher, tu ne mangeras pas de bonbons avant de dîner !

32 1. would pass **2.** if you had been hungry **3.** if it had not snowed **4.** will borrow

33 1. I would have come if you had invited me. **2.** I would stop complaining if you were nicer to me. **3.** I would help you if you asked me.

34 1. I will arrive on time if classes do not start before ten! **2.** I would have got a better mark if you had explained better! **3.** I would do another job if I didn't like your sense of humour so much!

35 1. c. **2.** a **3.** c

36 1. heard **2.** will play **3.** did not want **4.** had not yet cleaned the bathroom

37 1. When will Paul lend his phone? **2.** What will your parents do until they have retired? **3.** How long had Jim already been divorced when you met him?

38 1. I will help you write your application letter when you are more focused/ I will help you write your application letter as soon as I have wrapped up the presents.

PRONONCIATION

1 [èï] : cage, rage – [i] : cottage, message, manage, image, damage, sausage, advantage, vintage – [â] : camouflage, collage, mirage, sabotage. Ces mots sont des mots d'origine française. La règle est donc : la lettre **a** de la finale **-age** se prononce [â] dans les mots d'origine française !

2 [ᵉᵘt] : climate, desperate, delicate, senate, private, pirate, moderate – [èït] : to educate, to communicate, to hesitate

3 [tch] : chimney, challenge, cherry, chair, cheese – [k] : character, orchestra, architect, chaos, stomach, psychology, monarchy, chemistry, mechanic (tu sais maintenant que ces mots sont d'origine grecque !) – [ch] : chalet, chauffeur, champagne (pour ces trois là, tu t'en doutais sans doute, il sont français !)

4 1. hug ['Heug] **2.** huge ['Hioudj] **3.** cop ['kop] **4.** cope ['kᵉᵘoup] **5.** pin ['pin] **6.** pine ['païn] **7.** Sam ['sam] **8.** same ['sèïm] **9.** bit ['bit] **10.** bite ['baït] **11.** us ['eus] **12.** use ['iouz] **13.** win ['ouin] **14.** wine ['ouaïn] **15.** cut ['keut] **16.** cute ['kiout] **17.** mad ['mad] **18.** made ['mèïd] **19.** hat ['Hat] **20.** hate ['Hèït]

12 exceptions : **above, love, come, some, glove, oven.** Selon la règle, le o devrait se prononcer [ᵉᵘou] dans ces mots mais il se prononce [eu]. **mind, blind, kind** : selon la règle le i devrait se prononcer [i] dans ces mots mais il se prononce [aï]. **Cambridge** : le a devrait se prononcer [a]

mais se prononce [èï]. **have** : le **a** devrait se prononcer [èï] mais se prononce [a]. **to live** : le i devrait se prononcer [aï] mais se prononce [i] [à ne pas confondre avec l'adverbe **live** (*en direct*, pour une émission). Dans ce cas, le **i** se prononce bel et bien [aï].

5 a. Faux : il est souvent muet, comme dans les mots contenant -ght (indices : light ['laït] et although [ôl'DH^{eu}ou]). b. Faux, il peut se prononcer [eu] ou [ô] (indices : **blood** ['blèud] et **door** ['dô']). c. Faux, le son n'est pas toujours long, il est souvent court en fin de mot (indices : **honey** ['Heuni] et **monkey** ['monki]). d. Faux. Le ea peut en effet se prononcer [è] (**bread** ['brèd], **head** ['Hèd]) ou [i] (**bean** ['bin], **clean** ['klin]). Mais il peut se prononcer de plusieurs autres façons : [èï] (indice : **steak** ['stèïk]), [è^{eu}] (indice : **pear** ['pè^{eur}]), ou encore [â] (indice : **heart** ['Hât]). e. Hé non ! C'est surprenant mais il se prononce parfois [i] dans certains mots d'origine étrangère (souvent grecque). ex : **machette** [m^{eu}'chèti], **coyote** [coï '^{eu}outi], **recipe** ['rès^{eu}pi]. L'indice était le prénom **Penelope** [pi'nèl^{eu}pi]).

6 1. no ['grèït] ['tchit] 2. yes ['Hèd] ['brèd] 3. no ['grèït] ['mit] 4. no ['Hèd] ['Hât] 5. no ['bin] ['^{eu}ouch^{eur}] 6. no ['bè^{eur}] ['bïr] 7. no ['fi^{eur}] ['pè^{eur}] 8. yes ['ouè^{eur}] ['Hè^{eur}]

7 Le h est muet dans les mots en gras : 1. lighthouse ['laïtHaous] 2. happy ['Hapi] 3. vehicle ['vi-ik^{eul}] 4. ghost ['g^{eu}oust] 5. why ['ouaï] 6 . where ['ouè^{eur}] 7. heavy ['Hèvi] 8. **Thames** ['tèmz] 9. holidays ['Holidèïz] 10. behind [bi'Haïnd] 11. **heir** ['è^{eur}] 12. **honest** ['onist] 13. help ['Hèlp] Exceptions aux règles énoncées : **behind** [bi'Haïnd] (à l'intérieur d'un nom qui n'est pas composé mais le **h** se prononce), **heir** et **honest** (comme **hour**, cité dans la leçon).

8 [t] : missed, bumped, worked, looked, washed, hoped, mixed, picked, gossiped – [d] : retired, played, killed, applied, whispered, complained, whined, snowed, repaired – [^{eu}d]/[id] : ended, rated, expected

9 Sont mal accentués (bonne accentuation rétablie ici) : **a.** 'bookcase, 'character, 'ambulance, 'toothpaste, 'president, 'innocent, ma'roon, engi'neer, 'famous – **b.** to 'punish, to 'vary

10 He'llo, ba'nana, to'mato, po'tato, um'brella, No'vember, Ju'ly, e'leven, Sep'tember

11 Sont mal accentués (bonne accentuation rétablie ici) : a'daptable,

compre'hensible, 'cubism, e'xoticism, 'spacious, 'painter, a'ccepted, 'cavity, am'bition, collabo'ration

12 1. Curi'osity 'killed the 'cat! 2. My 'neighbour is 'friendly but he 'needs to im'prove his 'manners. 3. My 'sister's 'raincoat is 'gorgeous, isn't it? 4. Is your 'tablet 'under the 'sofa or 'on the 'sofa? 5. My 'mother-in-law has 'never 'sweetened her 'coffee. 6. I was 'born in Sep'tember and I'm a 'wonderful engi'neer! 7. The 'water on 'planes is not 'drinkable. 8. The 'German 'baby-sitter can't 'speak 'English. 9. My 'grandmother's got a lot of a'ffection for her Bur'mese 'cat.

13 schwa en gras : e'normous, 'sugar, to co'rrect, a'lone, edu'cation, im'portant, 'glorious, 'neighbour, a'mazing, a'genda, 'water, 'family, 'pasta, to for'give, 'lemon, I'talian, 'teacher, 'oven, 'expert, 'postman, a'bout, 'doctor, to a'djust, A'merican

14 1. Montante 2. Descendante 3. Descendante 4. Descendante 5. Descendante 6. Montante 7. Montante 8. Montante

15 Lettres muettes en gras : b muet dans : lam**b**, thum**b**, com**b**, dou**b**t – c muet dans : mus**c**le – d muet dans : han**d**kerchief – g muet dans : **g**nat – h muet dans : **h**eir, **h**onour – k muet dans : **k**nife – l muet dans : shou**l**d, ha**l**f – n muet dans : solem**n** – s muet dans : ai**s**le – w muet dans : whis**t**le – w muet dans : **w**rist, **w**hose

16 1. sugar 2. quiet 3. amazing 4. mistake 5. apologise 6. umbrella 7. music 8. My mother is German 9. Hello, I'm Dylan 10. Do you like chocolate? 11. Are you going to Simon's party?

17 1. 'kemɪst 2. griːn ʃɑːt 3. wi dɪd nɑt laɪk ðə pleɪ 4. ʃi haz biːn sɪk 'leɪtli 5. hiː brəʊk hiz 'glɑːsɪz lɑːst wiːk 6. hav jʊ siːn maɪ 'brʌðə? 7. ʃiː laɪkt riːdɪŋ wen ʃiː wəz ə tʃaɪld

CULTURE ET CIVILISATION

1 1. Wrong, he's a scholar in Oxford. 2. Right 3. Right 4. Wrong, it's the name of one of Eddie Izzard's stand up comedy shows 5. Wrong, they are famous in the whole world 6. Right 7. Right 8. Wrong, he thinks racist people are rude.

2 1. b. speech therapist 2. e. fifty 3. f. a stutter 4. a. Colin Firth 5. h. Blitz 6. d. Edward VIII 7. c. Wallis Simpson 8. g. Wembley

3 1. Germany 2. London 3. Lamp 4. Italy 5. Crimean 6. nurse 7. cholera

4 1. Busy (Kentucky) 2. Fair Play (California) 3. Simplicity (Virginia) 4. Badwater (California) 5. Boring (Oregon) 6. Happy Land (Oklahoma) 7. Darling (Mississippi) 8. Disappointment (Kentucky) 9. Rainbow (California) 10. Pillow (Pennsylvania) 11. Hammer (Dakota) 12. Hungry Horse (Montana)

5 1. Faux, cela signifie l'oublier l'espace d'un instant et s'en trouver mal à l'aise vis-à-vis de la personne. 2. Vrai 3. Faux, dans l'expression **Sorry for my tartle**, le terme est employé comme un nom.

6 1. Athens 2. London – sea 3. Rainy 4. Smoke 5. Fair

7 1. Vrai 2. Faux, au 17ème. 3. Faux, mais la chanson symbolise presque autant l'Irlande. 4. Faux, une statue de Molly a bien été installée sur Grafton Street, mais pour fêter les 1000 ans de la ville. 5. Vrai 6. Faux, elle est morte de la fièvre. 7. Vrai 8. Vrai 9. Faux, **'She was a fishmonger and sure it was no wonder/ For so were her father and mother before'** (ici so = *aussi*) 10. Vrai

8 1. Faux, il signifie insecte. 2. Faux, de l'université d'Harvard et de l'armée américaine. 3. Faux, elle s'attaque aux ordinateurs de la Bourse. 4. Faux, c'est une technologie d'origine suédoise. 5. Vrai

9 1. b 2. a 3. a 4. b 5. a

10 a. My kingdom for a horse! b. Something is rotten in the state of Denmark. c. There's method in my madness.

11 1. fair 2. tired 3. safe 4. break 5. live

12 1. b 2. b 3. b 4. c 5. c

13 mate (3), knackered (12), savage (13), gutted (11), ballistic (4), chav (6), It sucks (2), a weirdo (8), pissed off (10), fags (14), a Buck (1), broke (5), the bog (7), barf (9)

14 1. you 2. because 3. don't know 4. give me 5. going to 6. want to 7. What are you 8. a lot of 9. out of

15 1. isn't 2. am not 3. haven't 4. hasn't. **Ain't** est donc employé en argot en remplacement de **have** ou **to be**, à la forme négative.

Bravo, tu es venu à bout de ce cahier ! Il est temps à présent de faire le point sur tes compétences et de comptabiliser les icônes afin de procéder à l'évaluation finale. Reporte le sous-total de chaque chapitre dans les cases ci-dessous puis additionne-les afin d'obtenir le nombre final d'icônes dans chaque couleur. Puis découvre tes résultats !

GRAMMAIRE			
Unité 1			
Unité 2			
Unité 3			
Unité 4			
PRONONCIATION			
CULTURE ET CIVILISATION			
Total, tous chapitres confondus			

Tu as obtenu une majorité de...

Congratulations! Bravo !
Tu t'en es très bien sorti, continue comme ça !

Not bad at all! Ce n'est pas si mal ! Mais tu peux progresser en refaisant les exercices où tu as fait des erreurs.

Try again! Persévère !
Reprends l'ensemble de l'ouvrage en relisant bien les leçons avant de refaire les exercices.

Crédits iconographiques
Couverture : picto © DR
Intérieur : Shutterstock : ADE2013 : 105h (porte-cartes); Aleutie : 36bg; Alexander Ryabintsev : 74hd , 118b (guitare); Alexandra F : 17; Amplion : 47b; andromina : 48hd; angkrit : 37hd; Anna Frajtova : 15b; Annasunny24 : 26; Anthony Krikorian : 20h; Artisticco : 6h (poireaux), 14b (poireaux), 14b (salade); Azaze11o : 77d; Beresnev : 18b (pinceau), 86 (jardin); beta757 : 50h; bhjary : 113b; Blablo101 : 40hd, 70h, 116b; Bloomicon : 87bd; Bplanet : 93h, 99m, 118hg; bsd : 66md; Chattapat : 73md, 80b; chuhastock : 18b (masque); Colorcocktail : 100 (vin); Colorlife : 18h (pinceaux), 35, 51bd; Comodo777 : 117md; Creatarka : 18b (randonneur); createvil : 93b; Creative Stall : 18hd, 31bd, 87hd; Dacian G : 79bd; davorana : 19; Delices : 20b, 95m, 100b (poire); deviyanthi79 : 101bg (voiture); djdarkflower : 79md; Doremi : 71mg; eatcute : 68bd; Ecelop : 42bd; edel : 45b; ekler : 116 (papillons); Ellegant : 32bd; etraveler : 66hg; Evellean : 13hd (horloge), 81bd; Evgeniya Pushai : 72; Filip Bjorkman : 111b; filip robert : 118b; getfile : 43hd; GoodVector : 32h (pâtes), 64md, 80h; graphic-line : 58b, 75bg; GraphicsRF : 8h (miel), 14b (miel), 100b; grmarc : 110; gst : 6h (lait), 61b (camion); HelenStock : 54d; HieroGraphic : 62bd; Huza : 68mg; Iconic Bestiary : 40b, 41, 71hd; igorrita : 118b (manettes); Incomible : 6h (champignon),10hd, 14b (champignons), 14b (pomme), 15m, 21hd, 32hd, 115; Iurii Augulis : 67bd; jabkitticha : 70md; Jemastock : 101bg (phare); jesadaphorn : 59, 64h, 106hd, 112b, 119h; Julia Tim : 120bg; K N : 6m, 111m; Kachalova Kseniia : 109b; kamomeen : 4; karawan : 104h; La1n : 37bd; Laralova : 8h (sucre); LineTale : 63hd; Liudmila Dobraya : 103d; Lorelyn Medina : 81hd; lyeyee : 80m; Macrovector : 13b (chocolat), 31hd, 33b (chocolats), 44hd, 46, 50b, 57, 68hg, 71bd, 89, 91 (femme), 98bd (chocolat), 105h (tour Eiffel), 108b; MakaCz : 16h; Malchev : 100 (singe); Maquiladora : 12h (oiseau); Maria Kolyadina : 36hd; Maria Starus : 74bd; Marish : 24mg; mart : 98hd, 100b (jambon); Mascha Tace : 12h (brosse à dents), 18b (vélo), 24d, 60; Meder Lorant : 78m (étiquettes); Minur : 58hd; mirrra3 : 38b; Mix3r : 48md, 49b; mmar : 91 (soleil); Mushakesa : 8b, 9m, 9b, 13b (pêches), 14b (fruits); MyClipArtStore.com : 18b (tente), 111hd; mything : 6h (raisin), 6h (poire); Neti.OneLove : 93m; Nevena Radonja : 22h; Nikita Chisnikov : 42bg; nikiteev_konstantin : 102m; NotionPic : 15hd, 66m (sportifs), 114m; oakkii : 113h; Oceans : 104m, 116h (téléphone); Olga1818 : 9hd, 12 (couple), 21md, 39b, 42m, 75hd, 84, 118hd; olillia : 34, 61b, 114b; omnimoney : 96md; openeyed : 121; Osiv : 49hd, 100b (porte); Oxy_gen : 23, 67hd; Panda Vector : 18b (cavalier); Petityul : 38h; phloxii : 83bd; Pretty Vectors : 52g; primiaou : 108h; RATOCA : 28bg; Red monkey : 78bd (globe); red rose : 100b (tshirt); robuart : 90b; Rvector : 104b; Sashatigar : 76hg, 76bd, 102h; Sentavio : 11, 86 (chat), 119b; ShendArt : 18b (quilles); Sibiryanka : 44b; silanti : 6h (fromage); SlyBrowney : 13b (chips); Smart Design : 82, 88; stefanolunardi : 25b; SThom : 10b (pizza); stockakia : 30h (château); stockshoppe : 56; Studio Barcelona : 69; Studio_G : 51hd; Sudowoodo : 29; Sunny_nsk : 90hd; Syquallo : 16b; takiwa : 105b; Tomacco : 28h, 39hd, 66bg, 83md; vasabii : 77m, 99bd; Vector pro : 43bd, 103h, 109h; venimo : 102b; Virinaflora : 98b (maisons); Visual Generation : 25hd, 63bg, 101hd (visage); Vlada Young : 62hd; whanwhan.ai : 55; YANUSHEVSKAYA VICTORIA : 117hd; Yellowj : 65; yoshi-5 : 5, 12h (train), 22m, 53, 120hd; Zakharchenko Anna : 27, 30hg; zzveillust : 101bd; **Fotolia** : 12h (bain), 12h (veste), 78hd, 95hg; **DR** : 6h (crevette, huile et gaufre), 12h (rasoir), 13b (gaufre), 14b (crevettes), 18h (poubelle), 32hg, 33hd, 45h, 52b, 54g, 61h, 73h, 76hd, 85, 94, 96hd, 100 (sombrero), 101 (chapeau), 106b.

Conception graphique de l'intérieur : MediaSarbacane
Conception graphique de la couverture : AllRight
Adaptation graphique : Marion Huet
Mise en pages : Aurélia Monnier pour Céladon éditions
Réalisation : Céladon éditions, www.celadoneditions.com

Dépôt légal : mai 2017
N° d'édition : 4350
ISBN : 978-2-7005-8168-3

© 2017 Assimil
www.assimil.com
Imprimé Roumanie par Maste